30 Day Mediterranean Diet Meal Plan

Ultimate Weight Loss Plan With 100 Heart Healthy Recipes

SAMANTHA KEATING

Copyright © 2019 Samantha Keating

All rights reserved. No part of this publication may be reproduced, distributed, or transmitted in any form or by any means, including photocopying, recording, or other electronic or mechanical methods, without the prior written permission of the publisher, except in the case of brief quotations embodied in critical reviews and certain other noncommercial uses permitted by copyright law.

Limit of Liability/Disclaimer of Warranty: While the publisher and author have used their best efforts in preparing this book, they make no representations or warranties with respect to the accuracy or completeness of the contents of this book and specifically disclaim any implied warranties of merchantability or fitness for a particular purpose. No warranty may be created or extended by sales representatives or written sales materials. The advice and strategies contained herein may not be suitable for your situation. You should consult with a professional where appropriate. Neither the publisher nor author shall be liable for any loss of profit or any other commercial damages, including but not limited to special, incidental, consequential, or other damages.

ISBN: 9781077831230

DEDICATION

To health, wealth and a fulfilled life.

TABLE OF CONTENT

INTRODUCTION 1

WEEK 1 MEAL PLAN 4

WEEK 2 MEAL PLAN 6

WEEK 3 MEAL PLAN 8

WEEK 4 MEAL PLAN 10

BREAKFAST 13

    Toast With Salmon And Eggs 14

    Quinoa Breakfast Bake 15

    Egg Cups 16

    Egg Sandwich 19

    Spinach And Mushrooms Eggs 20

    Vegetable Egg Muffins 21

    Mediterranean Eggs 23

    Greek Scrambled Eggs 24

    Easy Eggs And Tomatoes 25

    Raspberry Avocado Smoothie 27

    Greek Bowl 27

    Potato And Chickpea Hash 29

    Omelet Casserole 31

    Feta Greek Yogurt 32

    Tuna Salad 33

    Oatmeal With Yogurt 35

    Vegetable Sushi 36

Breakfast Olive Salad 37

Banana Blueberries Smoothie 39

Date Almond Smoothie 39

Next Morning Bulgur With Blackberries 40

Goat Cheese Kale Frittata 41

Breakfast Pancakes 43

Feta And Vegetable Scrambled Eggs 44

Egg Salad 45

Quinoa Bowl 47

Honey Figs With Greek Yogurt 48

Mediterranean Overnight Oats 49

Avocado Toast 51

Greek Vegetable Pie 51

LUNCH 53

Citrus Herb Potatoes And Chicken 54

One Pan Chicken And Couscous 56

Zesty Chicken Soup 58

One Pot Mediterranean Pasta 61

Chicken Meatballs With Beans And Tomatoes 62

Crockpot Lentil Soup 63

Mediterranean Rice And Chickpea 66

Quinoa And Turkey 67

Shrimp Salad With Avocado 68

One Pan Cod 70

Greek Grain Salad 71

Pasta Salad 73

Mediterranean Farro Salad 75

Tuna Salad With Avocado And Yogurt Dressing 77

Tzatziki Turkey Meatballs 78

Greek Tacos With Vegetable Dressing.. 81

Chicken Pasta Salad 82

Crockpot Mediterranean Chicken 83

Flatbread Pizza... 84

Chopped Lunch Salad 87

Fish Tacos... 88

Souvlaki Bowl With Salmon 89

White Bean Salad... 92

Slow Cooker Chicken With Tomatoes And Artichokes 93

Eggplant Stuffed With Quinoa... 94

Garlic Shrimp 97

Orzo Lemon Chicken Soup... 98

Julienned Zucchini With Garlic Shrimp 99

Tuna And Beans 101

Barley Chicken Salad.. 102

DINNER 105

Slow Cooked Chicken And Orzo... 106

Mediterranean Chicken 107

One Pot Chicken And Lentils.. 109

One Pot Chicken Penne 112

Easy Mediterranean Pasta... 113

Chicken And Vegetables 115

Salmon And Tomatoes... 117

Mediterranean Cod 118

Slow Cooked Beef Stew 119

Greek Salad 122

Shrimp And Chickpeas Salad... 123

Crockpot Garlic Potatoes And Chicken 124

White Bean Kale Quinoa Soup 127

Salmon Olives And Veggies 128

Easy Prawns 129

Crab Salad 132

Mediterranean Quesadillas 133

Tangy Chicken Dinner 134

Vegetable Soup 136

Zucchini Chicken Soup 137

Mediterranean Chicken Sandwich 139

Spinach Grilled Cheese 141

Quinoa With Beans 142

Garlic Roasted Lamb Chops 144

Lentil Vegetable Soup 146

Vegetable Stir Fry 147

Penned With Asparagus, Leeks And Tomatoes 149

Roasted Chicken And Spinach Salad 151

Chickpea Vegetable Curry 153

Shrimp With Brown Rice 154

SNACKS & APPETIZERS 157

Easy Dip 158

Mediterranean Guacamole 159

Pistachios Bars 160

Fruity Almond Butter Oat Bars 162

Chocolate Cookie Snack Balls 163

Julienned Apple With Chocolate 164

Cinnamon Apple Chips.. 166

Garlic Herb Marinated Olives 167

Spicy Roasted Almonds... 168

Chicken Tenders With Herbs 169

INTRODUCTION

The Mediterranean diet is the natural way of eating of the people who live around the Mediterranean Sea. It has consistently been rated as the best out of other styles of eating. This is not really surprising because of the impressive array of health benefits that it provides which includes healthy heart, weight loss and disease prevention. The Mediterranean diet consists of natural foods, involves no calorie counting and is very easy to get used to.

The typical Mediterranean diet consist mainly of foods such as fish and other seafood, whole grains, vegetables, fruits, plant oils, nuts and seeds. These foods in their various capacities help to lower inflammation, improve the function of the cardiovascular system and strengthen the body against major diseases like diabetes, heart disease and even cancer.

Below are a few reasons to switch to the Mediterranean diet:

1. Better Heart Health

Researchers found out that people living in areas where the Mediterranean diet is eaten traditionally have better heart health. They have lower bad cholesterol levels and healthier circulatory systems. This was attributed to the lower consumption of processed sugars, red meat or other processed foods and the eating of a greater amount of vegetables, whole grains and seafood.

2. Slows Down Neurological Decline

Naturally, our bodies decline in several ways as we grow older. This decline can be accelerated or slowed down according to our lifestyles and the type of food we eat. The Mediterranean diet consists of a lot of anti-inflammatory foods that help to slow down degeneration of cells in the body, the brain and the nervous system. By slowing down neurological decline, normal mental function and quality of life can be maintained longer into old age. The risk of diseases such as Parkinson's and Alzheimer's and stroke are greatly reduced.

3. Higher Levels Of Omega-3 Fatty Acids

Following the Mediterranean diet can lead to a reduction in the risk factors of conditions like arthritis, dementia, depression, heart disease and some cancers. The greater amount of fish and seafood consumed results in higher levels of omega-3 which produces pro-health conditions in the body.

4. Healthy Weight Loss

The Mediterranean diet helps you to maintain a healthy body weight because it is devoid of fattening foods. If you are overweight, it will also help you to lose weight naturally over time. It makes it easy to lose weight without the burden of following a diet. The meals are rich in fiber and will help you to stay full longer and you will find it easier to resist unhealthy snacks.

5. Reduced Risk Of Diabetes

The very nature of the Mediterranean diet fortifies the body against the occurrence of type 2 diabetes. Whole grains, fruits and vegetables provide natural sugar and fiber and this reduces the likelihood of high blood glucose levels and insulin resistance. Even people who are already diagnosed with diabetes will benefit greatly by switching to the Mediterranean diet.

6. Reduction Of Stress Related Conditions

Recent research as shown that you may also enjoy a reduction of stress levels when you adopt the Mediterranean diet. This is greatly beneficial to people prone to depression and anxiety,

7. Longevity

The average lifespan of people in the Mediterranean regions is higher than those in Western nations. This difference has been attributed to the foods that they eat. The Mediterranean Diet provides a combination of foods that contribute to improved health and well being which subsequently results in a longer life.

The Mediterranean diet is the most natural diet you will ever find. It will improve your overall health without the usual burden of following a diet. There is no boredom with this diet because your plate will always be filled with fresh and colorful food. Whether you are a beginner or experienced dieter, this book has a compilation of 100 delicious recipes and a 4-week meal plan for you. The recipes are grouped into 30 Breakfasts, 30 Lunches, 30 Dinners and 10 Snacks. These recipes and meal plan will provide the help that you need to switch successfully from your present style of eating to the Mediterranean diet.

WEEK 1 MEAL PLAN

Day 1

Breakfast: *Toast With Salmon And Eggs*

Lunch: *Citrus Herb Potatoes And Chicken*

Dinner: *Slow Cooked Chicken And Orzo*

Snack: *Easy Dip* with crackers or potato chips

Day 2

Breakfast: *Quinoa Breakfast Bake*

Lunch: *One Pan Chicken And Couscous*

Dinner: *Mediterranean Chicken*

Snack: *Mediterranean Guacamole* with cucumbers

Day 3

Breakfast: *Egg Cups*

Lunch: *Zesty Chicken Soup*

Dinner: *One Pot Chicken And Lentils*

Snack: *Pistachios Bars*

Day 4

Breakfast: *Egg Sandwich*

Lunch: *One Pot Mediterranean Pasta*

Dinner: *One Pot Chicken Penne*

Snack: *Fruity Almond Butter Oat Bars*

Day 5

Breakfast: *Spinach And Mushrooms Eggs*

Lunch: *Chicken Meatballs With Beans And Tomatoes*

Dinner: *Easy Mediterranean Pasta*

Snack: *Chocolate Cookie Snack Balls*

Day 6

Breakfast: *Vegetable Egg Muffins*

Lunch: *Crockpot Lentil Soup*

Dinner: *Chicken And Vegetables*

Snack: *Julienned Apple With Chocolate*

Day 7

Breakfast: *Mediterranean Eggs*

Lunch: *Mediterranean Rice And Chickpea*

Dinner: *Salmon And Tomatoes*

Snack: *Cinnamon Apple Chips*

WEEK 2 MEAL PLAN

Day 1

Breakfast: *Greek Scrambled Eggs*

Lunch: *Quinoa And Turkey*

Dinner: *Mediterranean Cod*

Snack: *Garlic Herb Marinated Olives*

Day 2

Breakfast: *Easy Eggs And Tomatoes*

Lunch: *Shrimp Salad With Avocado*

Dinner: *Slow Cooked Beef Stew*

Snack: *Spicy Roasted Almonds*

Day 3

Breakfast: *Raspberry Avocado Smoothie*

Lunch: *One Pan Cod*

Dinner: *Greek Salad*

Snack: *Chicken Tenders With Herbs*

Day 4

Breakfast: *Greek Bowl*

Lunch: *Greek Grain Salad*

Dinner: *Shrimp And Chickpeas Salad*

Snack: Hummus With Pita Chips

Day 5

Breakfast: *Potato And Chickpea Hash*

Lunch: *Pasta Salad*

Dinner: *Crockpot Garlic Potatoes And Chicken*

Snack: Roasted Pumpkin Seeds

Day 6

Breakfast: *Omelet Casserole*

Lunch: *Mediterranean Farro Salad*

Dinner: *White Bean Kale Quinoa Soup*

Snack: Greek Yogurt With A Handful Of Berries

Day 7

Breakfast: *Feta Greek Yogurt*

Lunch: *Tuna Salad With Avocado And Yogurt Dressing*

Dinner: *Salmon Olives And Veggies*

Snack: Apple Slices With Almond Butter

WEEK 3 MEAL PLAN

<u>Day 1</u>

Breakfast: *Tuna Salad*

Lunch: *Tzatziki Turkey Meatballs*

Dinner: *Easy Prawns*

Snack: Pear Slices With Peanut Butter

<u>Day 2</u>

Breakfast: *Oatmeal With Yogurt*

Lunch: *Greek Tacos With Vegetable Dressing*

Dinner: *Crab Salad*

Snack: Tomato Slices With Feta Cheese

<u>Day 3</u>

Breakfast: *Vegetable Sushi*

Lunch: *Chicken Pasta Salad*

Dinner: *Mediterranean Quesadillas*

Snack: Whole-Wheat Crackers With Toamotoes And Goat Cheese

<u>Day 4</u>

Breakfast: *Breakfast Olive Salad*

Lunch: *Crockpot Mediterranean Chicken*

Dinner: *Tangy Chicken Dinner*

Snack: *Easy Dip* with pita chips or tortilla chips

<u>Day 5</u>

Breakfast: *Banana Blueberries Smoothie*

Lunch: *Flatbread Pizza*

Dinner: *Vegetable Soup*

Snack: *Mediterranean Guacamole* with carrots

Day 6

Breakfast: *Date Almond Smoothie*

Lunch: *Chopped Lunch Salad*

Dinner: *Zucchini Chicken Soup*

Snack: *Pistachios Bars*

Day 7

Breakfast: *Next Morning Bulgur With Blackberries*

Lunch: *Fish Tacos*

Dinner: *Mediterranean Chicken Sandwich*

Snack: *Fruity Almond Butter Oat Bars*

WEEK 4 MEAL PLAN

Day 1

Breakfast: *Goat Cheese Kale Frittata*

Lunch: *Souvlaki Bowl With Salmon*

Dinner: *Spinach Grilled Cheese*

Snack: *Chocolate Cookie Snack Balls*

Day 2

Breakfast: *Breakfast Pancakes*

Lunch: *White Bean Salad*

Dinner: *Quinoa With Beans*

Snack: *Julienned Apple With Chocolate*

Day 3

Breakfast: *Feta And Vegetable Scrambled Eggs*

Lunch: *Slow Cooker Chicken With Tomatoes And Artichokes*

Dinner: *Garlic Roasted Lamb Chops*

Snack: *Cinnamon Apple Chips*

Day 4

Breakfast: *Egg Salad*

Lunch: *Eggplant Stuffed With Quinoa*

Dinner: *Lentil Vegetable Soup*

Snack: Hummus With Pita Chips

Day 5

Breakfast: *Quinoa Bowl*

Lunch: *Garlic Shrimp*

Dinner: *Vegetable Stir Fry*

Snack: Roasted Pumpkin Seeds

Day 6

Breakfast: *Honey Figs With Greek Yogurt*

Lunch: *Orzo Lemon Chicken Soup*

Dinner: *Penned With Asparagus, Leeks And Tomatoes*

Snack: Greek Yogurt With A Handful Of Berries

Day 7

Breakfast: *Mediterranean Overnight Oats*

Lunch: *Julienned Zucchini With Garlic Shrimp*

Dinner: *Roasted Chicken And Spinach Salad*

Snack: Apple Slices With Almond Butter

BREAKFAST

Toast With Salmon And Eggs

Servings: 2

Prep time: 10 minutes

Cook time: 4 minutes

Ingredients:

3 ½ ounces of smoked salmon

½ avocado

2 slices whole wheat bread

2 eggs

1 tablespoon of thinly sliced scallions

1/4 teaspoon of freshly squeezed lemon juice

Worcester sauce

A pinch of cracked black pepper

A pinch of kosher salt

Microgreens

Directions:

1. Mash the avocado in a small bowl and combine thoroughly with salt and lemon juice.
2. Toast the bread and poach the eggs in boiling water.
3. Spread the avocado mixture on the two toasted bread slices then top with the salmon.
4. Add the poached eggs on the slices, carefully.
5. Season with cracked pepper and a drizzle of Worcester sauce.
6. Serve with a garnish of microgreens and scallions.

Nutrition per serving:

Calories: 211, fat: 13.3g, carbohydrates: 7.6g, proteins: 16.4g

Quinoa Breakfast Bake

This is a good meal to wake up to.

Servings: 8

Prep time: 10 minutes

Cook time: 1 hour 20 minutes

Ingredients:

3 cups of very ripe bananas, mashed

1 cup of uncooked quinoa

1/4 cup of slivered almonds

2 1/2 cups of unsweetened vanilla almond milk

1/4 cup of maple syrup or honey

1/4 cup of molasses

1 tablespoon of cinnamon

1 teaspoon of ground ginger

2 teaspoons of vanilla extract

1/2 teaspoon of ground allspice

1 teaspoon of ground cloves

1/2 teaspoon of salt

Directions:

1. In a casserole dish, thoroughly combine all the ingredients excluding the quinoa, almonds, and almond milk.

2. Stir in the quinoa until fully combined. Cover dish and chill in the refrigerator overnight.

3. The next morning, preheat the oven to 350°F.

4. Remove dish from refrigerator and give a good stir.

5. Use foil to cover dish and bake for about 60 to 75 minutes or until quinoa is dome and the liquid is fully absorbed.

6. Switch oven to broil, discard foil, sprinkle the almonds over the dish, pressing the almonds lightly into the mixture.

7. Broil on high for about 2-4 minutes or until almonds are golden brown.

Nutrition per serving:

Calories: 213, fat: 4g, carbohydrates: 41g, proteins: 5g

Egg Cups
This is one more reason to look forward to breakfast.

Servings: 6

Prep time: 15 minutes

Cook time: 25 minutes

Ingredients:

1 1/2 cups of chopped roasted bell peppers, rinsed, drained and pat dry

1 1/2 cups of chopped mushrooms

2/3 cup of plain almond milk

10 eggs

1/2 teaspoon of garlic powder

1/4 teaspoon of black pepper

1/8 teaspoon of salt

Goat cheese crumbles

Fresh basil leaves, torn

Directions:

1. Preheat oven to 350°F.

2. Coat a muffin pan with nonstick cooking spray.

3. Whisk the eggs, garlic powder, black pepper, milk and salt in a large bowl until fully combined.

4. Add in the bell pepper and mushrooms. Stir to combine.

5. Pour the egg mixture into each muffin cup and fill.

6. Bake for about 25 minutes or until set.

7. Cool for about 5-10 minutes before removing from pan.

8. Garnish with goat cheese and basil.

Nutrition per serving:

Calories: 168, fat: 13.8g, carbohydrates: 4.9g, proteins: 10.7g

18

Egg Sandwich

Servings: 1

Prep time: 5 minutes

Cook time: 3 minutes

Ingredients:

1 whole grain ciabatta roll, toasted

½ cup of roasted tomatoes

¼ cup of egg whites

1-2 Muenster cheese slices

1 tablespoon of pesto

1 teaspoon of olive oil

1 teaspoon of chopped fresh herbs

Salt

Pepper

Directions:

1. Heat the oil in a small skillet on medium heat.

2. Add the egg whites; season with the herbs, salt and pepper.

3. Cool for about 3-4 minutes or until egg is set; flip only once.

4. Spread pesto sauce on both halves of the bread roll.

5. Top the bottom half of the roll with the cooked egg; add the slices of cheese and tomatoes.

6. Cover with the other top half of the roll.

Nutrition per serving:

Calories: 458, fat: 24g, carbohydrates: 51g, proteins: 21g

Spinach And Mushrooms Eggs

This is quick and simple and fills you up.

Servings: 4

Prep time: 10 minutes

Cook Time: 10 minutes

Ingredients:

4 eggs

4 egg whites

2 cups of mushrooms, chopped

1/4 red onion, chopped

2 cups of fresh baby spinach, chopped

1/2 cup of low fat cheddar cheese, shredded

1/4 teaspoon salt

1/4 teaspoon ground black pepper

Olive oil cooking spray

Directions:

1. In a bowl, add together the eggs, egg whites, salt and pepper. Whisk well.

2. Coat a large skillet with cooking spray. Add onions and mushrooms then sauté with occasional stirring for about 3 minutes.

3. Add the chopped spinach then cook for about 1 minute, or until wilted.

4. Move the vegetables to the side of the skillet and add a little more cooking spray.

5. Pour eggs into the skillet and cook, occasionally stirring for about 3 minutes.

6. When the eggs are set, stir in the vegetables.

7. Sprinkle with the shredded cheese before serving.

Nutrition per serving:

Calories: 150, fat: 9g, carbohydrates: 5g, proteins: 14g

Vegetable Egg Muffins

Servings: 12

Prep time: 15 minutes

Cook time: 30 minutes

Ingredients:

2 cups of baby spinach, finely chopped

1 cup of crumbled feta cheese

1/2 cup of onion, finely chopped

1 cup of tomatoes, chopped or sliced

1 cup of cooked quinoa

1/2 cup of kalamata olives, pitted and chopped

8 eggs

1 tablespoon of chopped fresh oregano

1/4 teaspoon of salt

2 teaspoons of sunflower oil

Directions:

1. Preheat oven to 350°F.

2. Coat a 12-cup muffin pan with oil; set aside.

3. Heat a pan on medium heat; add oil and sauté the onions for 2 minutes.

4. Add the tomatoes; cook and stir for an additional minute.

5. Pour in the spinach; cook and stir for about 1 minute or until it wilts.

6. Remove from heat and add the oregano and olives; stir and keep aside.

7. Beat the eggs until fully combined (you can use a blender or mixer).

8. Add the cheese, salt, sautéed veggies, and quinoa to the eggs; whisk until fully incorporated.

9. Transfer the egg mixture into the prepared muffin pan.

10. Bake for 30 minutes or until eggs are lightly golden brown and done.

Nutrition per serving:

Calories: 114, fat: 7g, carbohydrates: 6g, proteins: 7g

Mediterranean Eggs

Theses pair well with crusty bread.

Servings: 6

Prep time: 5 minutes

Cook time: 1 hour 20 minutes

Ingredients:

2 tablespoons of extra virgin olive oil

1 1/2 large yellow onions, sliced

1/3 cup of firmly packed sun dried tomatoes, julienned

1 garlic clove, minced

6-8 large eggs

3 ounces of crumbled feta cheese

Freshly ground black pepper

Coarse kosher salt

Finely chopped parsley, optional

Directions:

1. Heat the oil in a large cast iron pan set on medium heat.

2. Add the onions and lower the heat until onions are just sizzling then cook for 1 hour until they are deep brown and soft. Stir the onions every 5-10 minutes.

3. Add the tomatoes and garlic; cook for about 2-3 minutes or until aromatic; stir constantly.

4. Spread out the sautéed veggies in an even layer and crack the eggs on top.

5. Sprinkle the cheese, salt and pepper on top.

6. Cover pan and cook for 10-15 minutes.

7. Garnish with parsley.

Nutrition per serving:

Calories: 183, fat: 11g, carbohydrates: 11g, proteins: 9g

Greek Scrambled Eggs

This is for mornings when you need a simple breakfast.

Servings: 2

Prep time: 10 minutes

Cook time: 7 minutes

Ingredients:

1 tablespoon of oil

2 spring onions, sliced

1 yellow pepper, diced

2 tablespoons of sliced black olives

1 tablespoon of capers

8 cherry tomatoes, quartered

4 eggs

1/4 teaspoon of dried oregano

Black pepper

Fresh parsley, optional

Directions:

1. In a pan, heat oil over medium heat and sauté the spring onions and pepper for some minutes until tender.

2. Add and sauté the capers, tomatoes and olives for an additional minute.

3. Break the eggs into the mixture; use a spatula or spoon to scramble immediately.

4. Season with the black pepper and oregano; stir constantly until eggs are done.

5. Garnish with parsley and serve.

Nutrition per serving:

Calories: 249, fat: 17g, carbohydrates: 13g, proteins: 14g

Easy Eggs And Tomatoes

You can eat this for breakfast or even for lunch.

Servings: 4

Prep time: 10 minutes

Cook time: 15 minutes

Ingredients:

1 tablespoon olive oil

2 cups of grape tomatoes, cut in halves

1 medium onion, chopped

2 tablespoons of sundried tomatoes, packed in oil, drained, chopped

4 eggs

4 egg whites

1/4 cup of reduced fat feta cheese

Directions:

1. Add the olive oil to a large skillet on medium heat. When the oil is hot, add cherry tomatoes and onions then cook and stir occasionally for 5 minutes.

2. Stir in the sun dried tomatoes and continue cooking and stirring occasionally until the vegetables are done.

3. In the meantime, spray cooking spray on another skillet and place it on medium heat. Beat eggs and egg whites together in a bowl (you can season with a little ground pepper if you like). Pour the beaten eggs into the skillet and cook until the eggs are set.

4. Divide the eggs equally among 4 plates. Scoop tomato mixture on top and then sprinkle with crumbled feta cheese.

Nutrition per serving:

Calories: 160, fat: 10g, carbohydrates: 7g, proteins: 12g

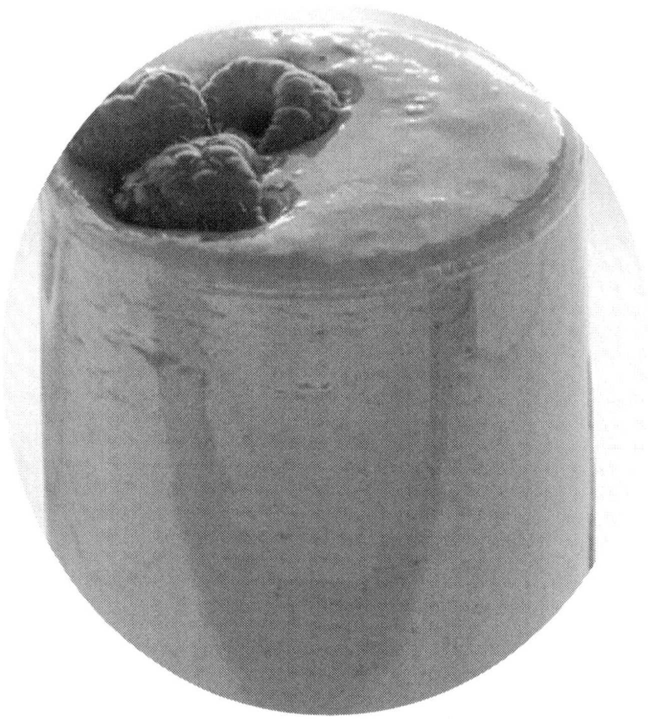

Raspberry Avocado Smoothie

Creamy avocado is nice and healthy inclusion in this smoothie.

Servings: 2

Prep time: 5 minutes

Cook time: minutes

Ingredients:

1 avocado, peeled, pitted

1/2 cup of frozen raspberries, (not thawed)

3/4 cup of raspberry juice

3/4 cup orange juice

Directions:

1. Add avocado, orange juice, raspberry juice and to a blender and puree until smooth.

Nutrition per serving:

Calories: 249, fat: 14g, carbohydrates: 32g, proteins: 3g

Greek Bowl

Servings: 2

Prep time: 10 minutes

Cook time: 20 minutes

Ingredients:

For the chickpeas:

1 (15-oz) can chickpeas, rinsed, drained, patted dry with paper towel

1 tablespoon of maple syrup, optional

1 tablespoon of shawarma spice blend

1 tablespoon of oil

1/4 teaspoon of sea salt

For serving:

1 batch of red pepper hemp tabbouleh

1/2 cup of cherry tomatoes, halved

1/2 cup of kalamata or green olives, pitted, chopped

3/4 cup of tzatziki

1 medium carrot, thinly sliced

1 medium cucumber, thinly sliced

Directions:

1. Preheat oven to 375°F.

2. In a bowl, toss all the chickpeas ingredients until combine.

3. Transfer the chickpeas to a baking sheet.

4. Bake for about 20-23 minutes or until the chickpeas are golden brown and a bit crisp. Set aside.

5. To serve, evenly divide all the serving ingredients between two bowls.

6. Add the chickpeas on top and drizzle fresh lemon juice over it.

Nutrition per serving:

Calories: 519, fat: 34.5g, carbohydrates: 49.8g, proteins: 12g

Potato And Chickpea Hash

Servings: 4

Prep time: 10 minutes

Cook time: 15 minutes

Ingredients:

2 cups of finely chopped baby spinach

4 cups of frozen shredded hash brown potatoes

1/2 onion, finely chopped

1 tablespoon minced fresh ginger

1 tablespoon curry powder

1/2 teaspoon salt

1/4 cup extra-virgin olive oil

1 (15-oz) can chickpeas, rinsed

1 medium zucchini, chopped

4 large eggs

Directions:

1. Combine onion, ginger, spinach, potatoes, curry powder and salt in a large bowl.

2. Heat the olive oil in a large skillet over medium-high heat then add the potato mixture and press into a layer. Cook for 3 to 5 minutes but don't stir, until golden brown at the bottom and crispy.

3. Reduce the heat to medium-low and then fold in zucchini and chickpeas. Break up the chunks of potato, until everything is just combined. Press back into an even layer.

4. Make 4 indentations in the mixture. Break the eggs into a cup one at a time and slip one into each indentation. Cover and continue to cook for 4 to 5 minutes or until the eggs are set.

Nutrition per serving:

Calories: 382, fat: 20g, carbohydrates: 37g, proteins: 14g

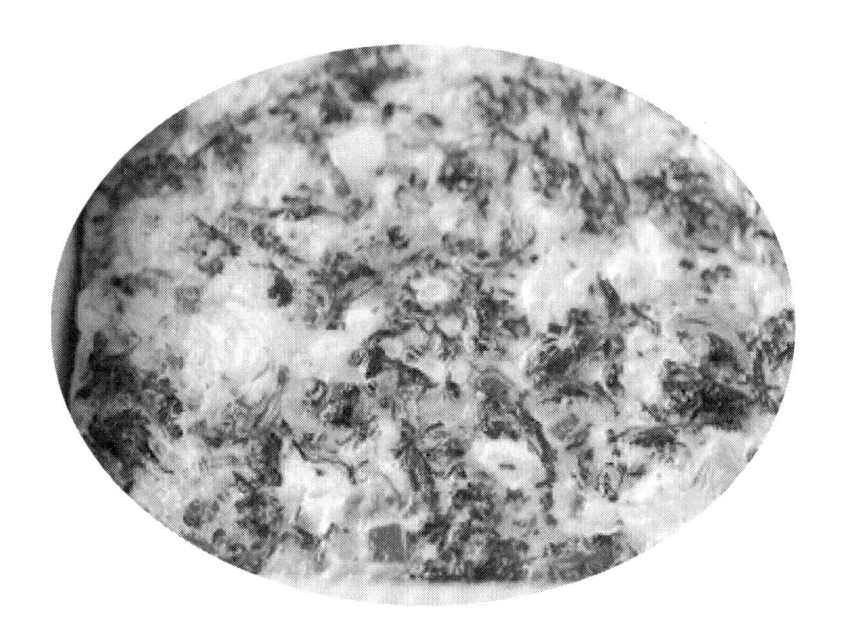

Omelet Casserole

This freezes quite well.

Servings: 12

Prep time: 10 minutes

Cook time: 35 minutes

Ingredients:

12 ounces of artichoke salad (with peppers and olives)

4 teaspoons of olive oil, divided

8 ounces of fresh spinach

2 garlic cloves, minced

2 cups of almond milk

12 large eggs

1 tablespoon of fresh chopped dill

1 teaspoon of lemon pepper

1 teaspoon of dried oregano

1 teaspoon of salt

5 ounces of sun dried tomato feta cheese, crumbled

Directions:

1. Preheat oven to 375°F. Grease a 9x13 baking dish with oil and set aside. Drain the artichoke salad and chop.

2. In a pan, heat 1 tablespoon of oil over medium heat and sauté the garlic and spinach for about 3 minutes until the spinach wilts.

3. Evenly layer the artichoke salad and sautéed spinach/garlic in the prepared pan.

4. Whisk the milk, lemon pepper, oregano, eggs, dill and salt together in a medium bowl.

5. Pour the milky mixture all over the veggies in the baking dish.

6. Sprinkle the cheese over everything.

7. Place pan in the middle of the oven and bake for about 35-40 minutes or until the center is firm.

Nutrition per serving:

Calories: 186, fat: 13g, carbohydrates: 5g, proteins: 10g

Feta Greek Yogurt

A bowl of nourishing creamy goodness.

Servings: 3

Prep time: 5 minutes

Cook time: 0 minutes

Ingredients:

1 cup of plain Greek yogurt

1 tablespoon of honey

1/2 cup of feta cheese

Directions:

1. Pulse the cheese, yogurt and honey in a blender or food processor until smooth.

2. Transfer to a wide container and keep in freezer until solid.

3. Remove from freezer and break into chunks.

4. Add some tablespoons of milk or water to a blender along with the frozen chunks.

5. Pulse until the mixture is creamy and smooth.

6. Drizzle with honey and serve.

Nutrition per serving:

Calories: 161, fat: 10g, carbohydrates: 11.8g, proteins: 6.6g

Tuna Salad

Eat this light breakfast on days when you need to move around a lot.

Servings: 2

Prep time: 8 minutes

Cook time: 0 minutes

Ingredients:

1 can Albacore white tuna, drained

1/4 cup roasted red peppers diced

8 kalamata olives sliced

2 tablespoons of capers

2 tablespoons of olive oil

1 tablespoon of lemon juice

1 tablespoon of chopped fresh flat-leaf parsley optional

Pepper

Salt, optional

Directions:

1. In a bowl, add all the ingredients.

2. Break the tuna apart with a fork and combine everything together.

Nutrition per serving:

Calories: 155, fat: 16g, carbohydrates: 2g, proteins: 0g

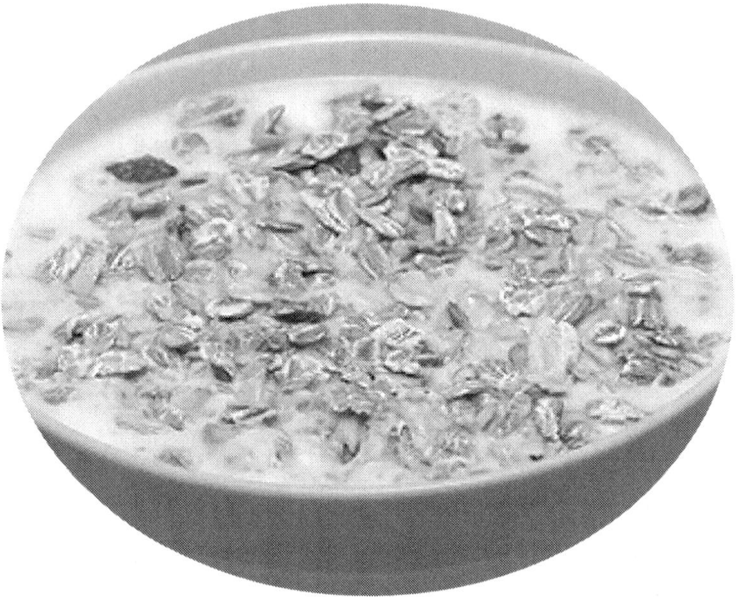

Oatmeal With Yogurt

This simple breakfast is so lovable.

Servings: 2

Prep time: 5 minutes

Cook time: 0 minutes

Ingredients:

2 cups of cooked oatmeal

1 1/2 cups almond milk with vanilla

1 teaspoon vanilla essence

1 1/2 cups Greek yogurt

1 teaspoon chia seeds

1 teaspoon flaxseed seeds

1 teaspoon lemon juice

25 drops stevia

Directions:

1. Mix all the ingredients together in a large bowl, except the yogurt.

2. Divide the mixture into 2 cups.

3. Add half of the yogurt to each cup and mix.

4. Serve right away.

Nutrition per serving:

Calories: 87, fat: 2g, carbohydrates: 24g, proteins: 1g

Vegetable Sushi

Servings: 10

Prep time: 10 minutes

Cook time: 0 minutes

Ingredients:

1 cucumber, ends trimmed then thinly sliced lengthwise

1/4 cup of crumbled feta cheese

1/4 cup of finely diced red onion

1/2 bell pepper, finely diced

For the tzatziki sauce:

1/2 cup of plain greek yogurt

1 clove garlic, minced

2 teaspoon of lemon juice

1 teaspoon of fresh dill, chopped

Pepper

Salt

Directions:

1. Pat dry the thin cucumber slices in-between layers of paper towels then set aside.
2. Combine all the tzatziki ingredients together to make the sauce.
3. Spread some of the sauce onto each slice of cucumber.
4. Divide the cheese, onion and pepper evenly on top of the cucumber slices. Roll up each one and use a toothpick to secure.

Nutrition per serving:

Calories: 54, fat: 2.2g, carbohydrates: 5.2g, proteins: 4g

Breakfast Olive Salad

This tasty salad is packed with nutrients.

Servings: 2

Prep time: 15 minutes

Cook time: 0 minutes

Ingredients:

For the salad:

1 red or white onion, chopped

1 teaspoon sumac

1/4 teaspoon salt

1 cup green olives, pitted

1 cup grape tomatoes, halved

1/4 cup fresh dill, chopped

¼ cup parsley, chopped

1 green onion, chopped, optional

For the dressing:

2 tablespoons of olive oil

1 tablespoon of lemon juice, freshly squeezed

1 tablespoon of pomegranate molasses

Directions:

1. Combine the sumac, onion and salt in a medium bowl the use your hands to mix well until evenly coated with sumac and salt.

2. Add the tomatoes, dill, onions, parsley and olives then toss.

3. In a small container, whisk the dressing ingredients together then drizzle this mixture over the salad.

4. Thoroughly stir to combine.

Nutrition per serving:

Calories: 213, fat: 14.7g, carbohydrates: 21.3g, proteins: 2.6g

Banana Blueberries Smoothie

Sometimes, it's good to simply drink your breakfast.

Servings: 1

Prep time: 5 minutes

Cook time: 0 minutes

Ingredients:

1 ½ cup of blueberries

1 cup of almond milk

½ banana, peeled and chopped

Directions:

1. Pulse all the ingredients in a blender until smooth.

Nutrition per serving:

Calories: 729, fat: 58.2g, carbohydrates: 58.3g, proteins: 7.8g

Date Almond Smoothie

Servings: 1

Prep time: 5 minutes

Cook time: 0 minutes

Ingredients:

1 ½ cups of unsweetened almond milk

½ cup of medjool dates, pitted

1 cup of ice cubes

2 tablespoons of almond butter

1 small banana

1 tablespoon of honey, optional

Directions:

1. Mix the dates and milk in a medium bowl; cover and refrigerate overnight.

2. To serve, pulse the dates/milk mixture along with the remaining ingredients in a blender until smooth.

Nutrition per serving:

Calories: 429, fat: 5g, carbohydrates: 85g, proteins: 6g

Next Morning Bulgur With Blackberries
This gives you something to look forward to.

Servings: 2

Prep time: 5 minutes

Cook time: 0 minutes

Ingredients:

¼ cup of bulgur

¼ cup of blackberries

⅔ cup of plain Greek yogurt or low-fat yogurt

3 tablespoons of milk

1/4 teaspoon of ground ginger

2 tablespoons of honey

Directions:

1. Combine all the ingredients, except the blackberries, in a bowl.

2. Evenly divide the mix between two mason jars.

3. Add the blackberries as toppings.

4. Cover jar and refrigerate overnight. You can keep it in the fridge for up to 2 days.

5. Stir and serve.

Nutrition per serving:

Calories: 215, fat: 1g, carbohydrates: 45g, proteins: 8g

Goat Cheese Kale Frittata
This is just divine.

Servings: 6

Prep time: 5 minutes

Cook time: 15 minutes

Ingredients:

1 medium onion, halved and thinly sliced

2 cups of fresh kale, roughly torn

2 teaspoons of olive oil

4 egg whites

6 eggs

$\frac{1}{8}$ teaspoon of ground black pepper

$\frac{1}{4}$ teaspoon of salt

1 ounce of goat cheese, crumbled

$\frac{1}{4}$ cup of oil-packed dried tomatoes, drained, thinly sliced

Directions:

1. Preheat your broiler.

2. In a medium skillet, heat oil on medium heat then sauté the onion and kale for about 10 minutes or until onion is softened.

3. Whisk the egg whites, egg, pepper and salt in a medium bowl; pour this mixture into the pan.

4. Reduce heat to medium low and cook.

5. Gently lift the egg mix at the edges with a spatula so that every uncooked part is heated.

6. Sprinkle with the cheese and dried tomatoes.

7. Transfer to the oven and broil for 1-2 minutes or until eggs are done.

8. Divide into wedges and serve.

Nutrition per serving:

Calories: 145, fat: 4g, carbohydrates: 6g, proteins: 11g

Breakfast Pancakes

Servings: 2

Prep time: 10 minutes

Cook time: 3 minutes

Ingredients:

2 bananas, peeled, chopped

4 eggs

1 tablespoon of milled flax seeds

1 tablespoon of bee pollen, milled

½ teaspoon of extra virgin olive oil

Directions:

1. In a bowl, crack the eggs and add the flaxseeds, bee pollen and banana; blend with a hand mixer until smooth.

2. In a nonstick pan set on medium heat, heat a little oil and pour some of the banana mixture into it.

3. Cook for about 2 minutes or until the pancake is golden at the bottom and can be lifted easily.

4. Flip with a spatula and cook for another 30 seconds; transfer to a plate.

5. Repeat process for remaining batter.

Nutrition per serving:

Calories: 132, fat: 5.1g, carbohydrates: 15.6g, proteins: 7g

Feta And Vegetable Scrambled Eggs

This comes together very easily.

Servings: 1-2

Prep time: 2 minutes

Cook time: 4 minutes

Ingredients:

3 eggs

1 cup of baby spinach

1/3 cup of tomato, diced and seeded

2 tablespoons of feta cheese, cubed

1 tablespoon of vegetable oil

Pepper

Salt

Directions:

1. In a pan, heat oil on medium heat and cook the spinach and tomatoes until spinach wilts.

2. Stir in the eggs and scramble for 30 seconds.

3. Add the cheese and continue cooking until egg is done.

4. Add salt and pepper to taste.

Nutrition per serving:

Calories: 128, fat: 8.7g, carbohydrates: 2.6g, proteins: 10.3g

Egg Salad

The leftovers keep well in the refrigerator.

Servings: 4

Prep time: 5 minutes

Cook time: 0 minutes

Ingredients:

8 large hardboiled eggs, chopped

1/2 cup of plain Greek yogurt

1/2 cup of red onion, finely chopped

1/2 cup of chopped sun-dried tomatoes, drained

1/4 cup of olives, chopped

1/2 cucumber, chopped

1 1/2 teaspoons of oregano

1/2 teaspoon of sea salt

1/4 teaspoon of cumin

A splash of lemon juice

Freshly ground black pepper

Directions:

1. In to a bowl, combine the chopped eggs with red onion, tomatoes, olives and cucumber.

2. Add the lemon juice, spices and yogurt then stir together.

Nutrition per serving:

Calories: 244, fat: 18g, carbohydrates: 8g, proteins: 11g

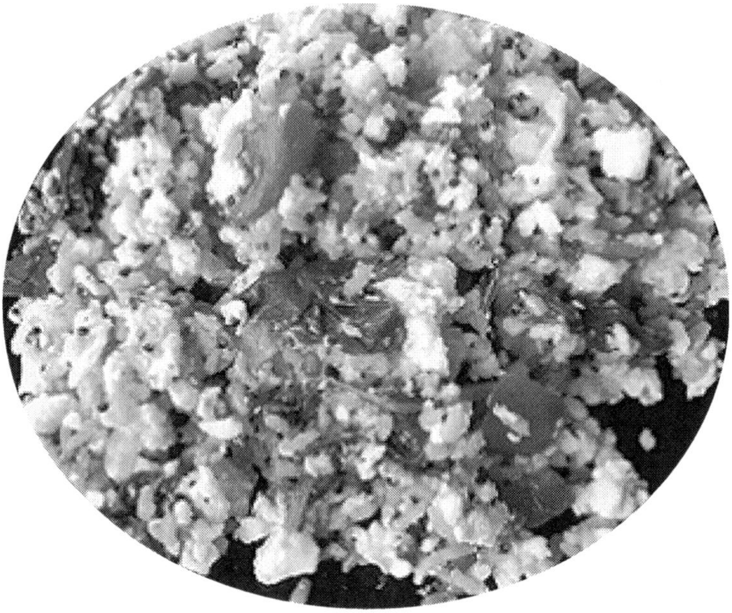

Quinoa Bowl

Spice up your everyday eggs with this recipe.

Servings: 6

Prep time: 5 minutes

Cook time: 13 minutes

Ingredients:

12 eggs

1 teaspoon of onion powder

1 teaspoon of granulated garlic

½ teaspoon of pepper

½ teaspoon of salt with

¼ cup of plain Greek yogurt

1 teaspoon of olive oil

1 (5-oz) bag of baby spinach

2 cups of cherry tomatoes, halved

2 cups of cooked quinoa

1 cup of feta cheese

Directions:

1. Whisk the eggs, onion powder, garlic, yogurt, pepper and salt in a large bowl. Set aside.

2. Heat the oil in a large skillet and cook the spinach for about 3-4 minutes, or until it wilts slightly.

3. Stir in the tomatoes and continue to cook for about 3-4 minutes until tomatoes are tender.

4. Stir in the egg/yogurt mix then cook for about 7-9 minutes until eggs are done.

5. Stir in the quinoa and feta then allow to heat through.

Nutrition per serving:

Calories: 357, fat: 20g, carbohydrates: 20g, proteins: 23g

Honey Figs With Greek Yogurt

Servings: 4

Prep time: 5 minutes

Cook time: 5 minutes

Ingredients:

8 ounces of fresh figs, halved

1 tablespoon of honey

1/4 cup of chopped pistachios

2 cups of plain low-fat Greek yogurt

A pinch of ground cinnamon

Directions:

1. In a medium pan, heat the honey on medium heat.

2. Add the figs, with cut side facing down and cook for about 5 minutes, or until caramelized.

3. Serve the yogurt, topped with honey figs and the rest of the ingredients.

Nutrition per serving:

Calories: 237, fat: 4.3g, carbohydrates: 41.2g, proteins: 12.7g

Mediterranean Overnight Oats

Servings: 1

Prep time: 5 minutes

Cook time: 0 minutes

Ingredients:

1/2 cup of oats

1/4 teaspoon of cinnamon

1/4 teaspoon of cardamom

1 teaspoon of chia seeds

1 packet of truvia

1/4 cup of yogurt

1/2 cup of almond milk

2 large medjool dates chopped

2 tablespoons of chopped walnuts

1 teaspoon of date molasses

1 teaspoon of tahini paste

Directions:

1. In a small bowl, mix the oats, cardamom, cinnamon, chia seeds, truvia and dates together.

2. Stir in the yogurt and almond milk then chill overnight in the fridge.

3. Stir in the morning and top with the remaining ingredients.

Nutrition per serving:

Calories: 468, fat: 15g, carbohydrates: 77g, proteins: 11g

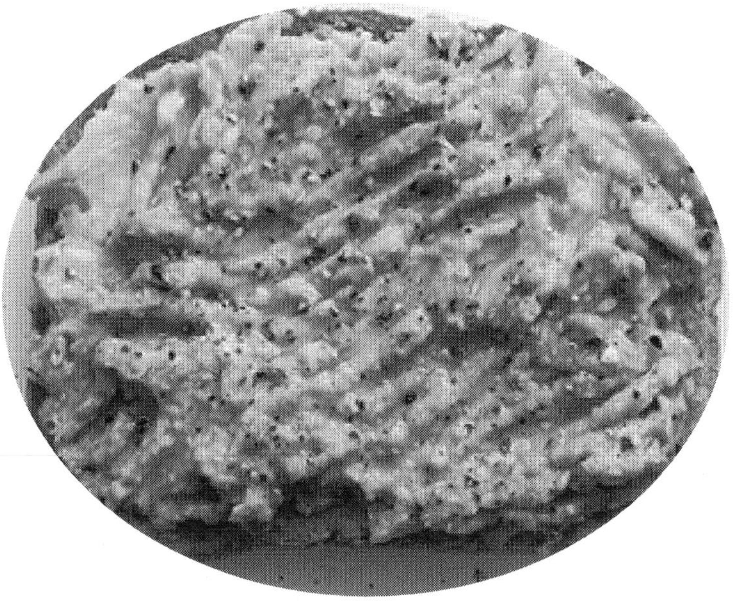

Avocado Toast

A very light breakfast for when you are on the go.

Servings: 1

Prep time: 5 minutes

Cook time: 1 minute

Ingredients:

2 slices of whole wheat bread

1 avocado

Salt, to taste

Pepper, to taste

Directions:

1. Heat up a frying pan and fry the bread for 1 minute.

2. Blend the avocado very well and add salt and pepper to the taste.

3. Put the avocado mix on the bread slices and serve right away.

Nutrition per serving:

Calories: 140, fat: 16g, carbohydrates: 7.8g, proteins: 2g

Greek Vegetable Pie

Servings: 4

Prep time: 10 minutes

Cook time: 25 minutes

Ingredients:

7 cups spring mix salad greens

1 medium yellow onion, chopped finely

1/3 cup of extra virgin olive oil

4 large egg, lightly beaten

1/8 teaspoon of black pepper

1/8 teaspoon of sea salt

1/2 cup of crumbled feta cheese

Directions:

1. Preheat oven to 356°F. Coat a flan dish with nonstick cooking spray.

2. In a large pan, heat oil on medium heat and cook the onions until opaque.

3. Stir in the greens then cook and stir until wilted.

4. Add salt and pepper to taste.

5. Transfer the mixture to the flan dish and sprinkle with the feta cheese then pour the eggs on top.

6. Bake for about 20 minutes or until egg is browned lightly and well cooked.

Nutrition per serving:

Calories: 325, fat: 27.9g, carbohydrates: 7.3g, proteins: 11.2g

LUNCH

Citrus Herb Potatoes And Chicken

Servings: 4

Prep time: 10 minutes

Cook time: 45 minutes

Ingredients:

4 chicken thighs, skin-on, bone-in

8 baby potatoes, halved

1 red bell pepper, deseeded and cut into wedges

1 red onion, cut into wedges

1 large zucchini, sliced

3 tablespoons of olive oil, divided

1 tablespoon of red wine vinegar

2 teaspoons of dried oregano

4 garlic cloves, crushed

2 teaspoons of dried parsley

3 teaspoons of dried basil

¼ cup of lemon juice

2 teaspoons of salt

Slices of lemon

4 tablespoons of kalamata olives, pitted

Directions:

1. Mix the vinegar, oregano, garlic, parsley, lemon juice, basil, salt and 2 tablespoons of oil in a shallow dish. Divide the mixture into half and reserve one part in a jug.

2. Pat the chicken dry and add to the dish; coat it evenly in the marinade. Cover and leave to marinate for at least 1 hour or overnight. Occasionally turn the chicken in the marinade.

3. Preheat oven to 430°F.

4. In a large cast iron skillet, heat the rest of the oil on medium high heat.

5. Brown the chicken for about 4 minutes per side. Drain the excess fat, leaving just about 1 tablespoon in the pan.

6. Add the veggies by arranging them around the pieces of chicken.

7. Drizzle the reserved marinade on the vegetables and toss to coat then cover the skillet with foil.

8. Bake for about 35 minutes, or until chicken is well cooked and the potatoes are tender.

10. Switch oven to broil on medium heat; uncover skillet and cook for an additional 5-10 minutes or until the potatoes and chicken are golden brown and crisp.

11. Garnish with slices of lemon and olives.

Nutrition per serving:

Calories: 572, fat: 22g, carbohydrates: 71.4g, proteins: 27.1g

One Pan Chicken And Couscous

Servings: 4

Prep time: 15 minutes

Cook time: 23 minutes

Ingredients:

2 pounds of boneless, skinless chicken breast

2 tablespoons of olive oil

3/4 teaspoon of kosher salt, divided

1/4 teaspoon of ground black pepper

1 red bell pepper, chopped into 1 inch pieces

1/2 red onion, chopped into 1 inch pieces

1/2 teaspoon of dried oregano

1/4 teaspoon of dried thyme

1 garlic clove

1 (5.1oz) jar of capers, drained, rinsed

2 cups of chicken broth

1 cup of uncooked couscous

1/2 lemon, juiced

1/3 cup of crumbled feta cheese

3/4 cup of diced tomatoes

1/4 cup of pine nuts, toasted

2 tablespoons of minced fresh parsley

Directions:

1. Heat the oil in a large skillet over medium high heat.

2. Add the chicken and season with pepper and ½ teaspoon of salt. Cook for 4 minutes per side until browned.

3. Push the meat to one side of the pan and turn down heat to medium.

4. Add the onions, peppers, oregano, thyme and ¼ teaspoon of salt; cook for an additional 4 minutes with frequent stirring.

5. Add the garlic and cook for about 1 minute until aromatic; stir constantly. Transfer the chicken to a plate.

6. Stir in the broth, couscous and capers then turn up heat to medium high.

7. When the sauce starts boiling, return the chicken to the pan and ensure it is covered with the sauce.

8. Cover the pan, lower heat to medium and cook for 8-10 minutes or until the chicken is well cooked and the couscous is soft.

9. Pour the lemon juice on top.

10. Garnish with parsley, cheese, tomatoes and pine nuts.

Nutrition per serving:

Calories: 522, fat: 28g, carbohydrates: 22g, proteins: 54g

Zesty Chicken Soup

Servings: 8

Prep time: 20 minutes

Cook time: 1 hour 20 minute

Ingredients:

3 pounds chicken breasts, bone-in

3 tablespoons of olive oil, divided

2 teaspoons taco seasoning

1 large onion, diced

6 garlic cloves, minced

2 jalapeno peppers, diced

1 poblano pepper, diced

1 (28-oz) can tomatoes

8 cups of chicken stock

1 cup of cilantro, chopped

Juice of 2 limes

Fresh avocado and cilantro for garnish

Directions:

1. Preheat your oven to 375°F.

2. In a large sheet, arrange the chicken breasts, drizzle with 1 tablespoon of oil then sprinkle with the taco seasoning.

3. Place in the oven and cook for 30-45 minutes, or until cooked through. Chop the cooked chicken into pieces.

4. In the meantime, add the remaining 2 tablespoons of oil to a large pot and heat on medium heat. Add the onions and cook for about 5-6 minutes, or until translucent.

5. Add garlic and peppers. Cook and stir for about 1-2 minutes or until fragrant.

6. Stir in the tomatoes and chicken stock. Set the heat to medium and bring to a boil.

7. Stir in the chicken, lime juice and cilantro. Taste and add salt or pepper as desired.

8. Serve with fresh cilantro and avocado.

Nutrition per serving:

Calories: 280, fat: 11g, carbohydrates: 16g, proteins: 27g

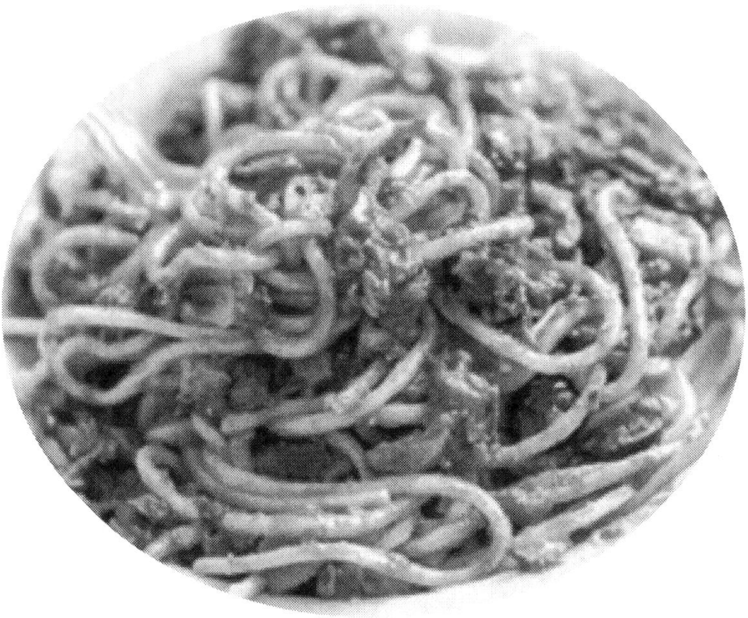

One Pot Mediterranean Pasta

Servings: 4

Prep time: 10 minutes

Cook time: 15 minutes

Ingredients:

3 cups of water

1 (8 ounce) package of whole grain pasta

1 can of fire roasted tomatoes

1 can of vegetable broth

1 can of artichoke hearts drained

1/2 purple onion sliced

1 cup of black olives

1 teaspoon of dried thyme

1 teaspoon of cumin

Sea salt

Black pepper

Basil, optional

Parmesan, optional

Directions:

1. In a large pot, boil water and add pasta, tomatoes, broth, cumin, artichoke, thyme, onions, and olives.

2. Bring to a boil on high heat and stir gently to combine.

3. Slightly lower heat to a simmer and use tongs to stir occasionally to prevent the pasta from sticking to the bottom of the pot or sticking together.

4. Once the liquid has thickened, add salt and pepper to taste. Continue cooking until pasta is done then scoop unto a plates.

5. Garnish with cheese or fresh herbs and serve.

Nutrition per serving:

Calories: 196, fat: 14g, carbohydrates: 14g, proteins: 2g

Chicken Meatballs With Beans And Tomatoes

This is another delicious one pan dish for lunch or dinner.

Servings: 4

Prep time: 10 minutes

Cook time: 20 minutes

Ingredients:

1 pound of ground chicken

2 tablespoons of fresh rosemary, chopped

2 egg whites

1/4 cup of fat-free feta cheese, crumbled

1/4 cup of whole wheat panko bread crumbs

1/4 cup of fresh parsley, chopped

1 tablespoon of olive oil

1 (15-oz) can of chickpeas, rinsed and drained

1 cup of grape or cherry tomatoes

3 garlic cloves, chopped roughly

1/2 teaspoon of kosher salt

Directions:

1. Preheat your oven to 400°F. Coat a baking pan with nonstick cooking spray.

2. Combine the rosemary, egg white, cheese, ground chicken, parsley, and panko in a bowl until well mixed. Set aside.

4. Mix the oil, chickpeas, garlic, tomatoes, and salt in another bowl thoroughly. Spread this mixture in the prepared pan in an even layer.

5. Use your hands to form the ground chicken mix into 2-inch balls and arrange on the tomatoes/beans mixture.

6. Bake for 15-20 minutes or until the meatballs are thoroughly cooked and firm.

Nutrition per serving:

Calories: 398, fat: 18g, carbohydrates: 30g, proteins: 31g

Crockpot Lentil Soup

Simply put everything together and let your slow cooker do all the work.

Servings: 6

Prep time: 5 minutes

Cook time: 7 hours

Ingredients:

5 cups of vegetable broth

3 cups of fresh baby spinach

1 cup of green lentils, rinsed

1/2 cup of celery, thinly chopped

1/2 cup of red onion, thinly chopped

1/2 cup of carrot, peeled and thinly chopped

3 cloves of garlic, minced

1 small sweet potato, peeled and thinly chopped

2 tablespoons of tomato paste

2 tablespoons of dried oregano

2 teaspoons of lemon juice

1 teaspoon of lemon zest

1/2 teaspoon of ground cumin

Directions:

1. Mix all the ingredients together, excluding the spinach and tomato paste, in a crockpot.

2. Cook for 3-4 hours on high or 6-8 hours on low.

3. Once time is up and the lentils are soft, add the tomato paste and spinach; stir to combine.

4. Cover pot and cook on high for an additional 20 minutes or until the spinach wilts.

Nutrition per serving:

Calories: 149, fat: 1g, carbohydrates: 29g, proteins: 9g

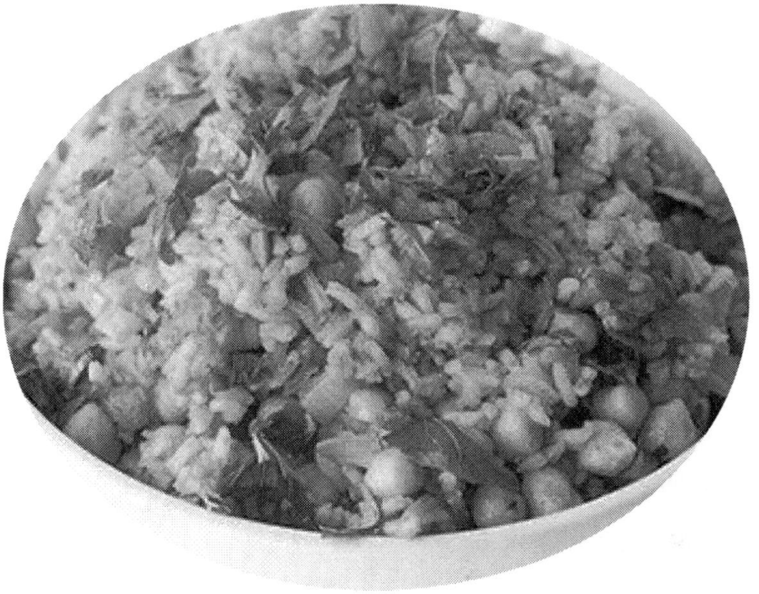

Mediterranean Rice And Chickpea

This cooks really quickly.

Servings: 6

Prep time: 10 minutes

Cook time: 15 minutes

Ingredients:

3 cups of cooked brown rice

1 (14 ounce) can of chickpeas, drained and rinsed

2 garlic cloves, minced

1 medium red onion, thinly chopped

1 teaspoon of no sugar added tomato paste

1/2 cup of roasted red peppers, thinly chopped

3 teaspoons of dried oregano leaves

1/2 cup of nonfat feta cheese crumbles

1 lemon, cut into 4 wedges

1 small roma tomato, thinly chopped

1 tablespoon of olive oil

Directions:

1. Heat the oil in a large skillet on medium heat and sauté the onion, garlic and chickpeas until onion is tender; stir often.

2. Add the rice, tomato paste, oregano and roasted red pepper. Cook and stir frequently until heated through.

3. Scoop into serving dishes and garnish with cheese and tomato.

4. Drizzle with a squeeze of lemon juice and serve

Nutrition per serving:

Calories: 269, fat: 8g, carbohydrates: 42g, proteins: 9g

Quinoa And Turkey

Servings: 4

Prep time: 10 minutes

Cook time: 20 minutes

Ingredients:

2 cups of cooked turkey, cut into 1 inch chunks

1 tablespoon of extra virgin olive oil

1 small yellow onion, sliced

2 garlic cloves, minced

1 cup of low sodium chicken broth

1 1/2 cups of quinoa, rinsed in cool water

1 (14-oz) can of diced tomatoes

2 cups of spinach, chopped

1/2 cup of low fat feta cheese, crumbled

1/2 teaspoon of kosher salt

Directions:

1. Heat the oil in a large skillet on medium heat and sauté the onion and garlic until onion starts to soften.

2. Add the turkey, broth, quinoa, tomatoes and salt; stir and allow to come to a boil.

3. Lower heat to a simmer and stir in the spinach.

4. Cook until the broth is absorbed, stirring occasionally to keep the quinoa from sticking to the bottom.

5. Serve in bowls and garnish with feta cheese.

Nutrition per serving:

Calories: 117, fat: 8g, carbohydrates: 8g, proteins: 5g

Shrimp Salad With Avocado

Fresh shrimp salad with tomato and avocado.

Servings: 4

Prep time: 20 minutes

Cook time: minutes

Ingredients:

1 pound cooked salad shrimp

2 tomatoes, diced

2 avocados, peeled, pitted, sliced thickly

1 small sweet onion, chopped

Salt, to taste

Pepper, to taste

2 tablespoons lime juice

Directions:

1. In a large bowl, combine avocados, onion, tomatoes and shrimp.

2. Season with salt and pepper then gently mix well.

3. Drizzle with lime and give a final stir. Serve and enjoy.

Nutrition per serving:

Calories: 230, fat: 11g, carbohydrates: 17g, proteins: 31g

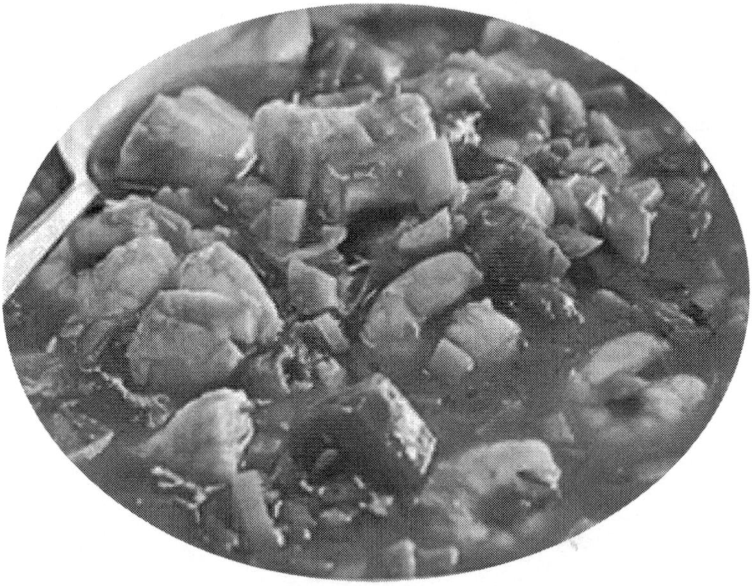

One Pan Cod

This is classic Mediterranean cuisine.

Servings: 4

Prep time: 5 minutes

Cook time: 30 minutes

Ingredients:

1 pound of cod, cut into 4 pieces

2 tablespoons of olive oil

1 small onion sliced

3 garlic cloves, chopped

2 cups of sliced fennel

1 (14.5-oz) can of diced tomato

1 cup of diced fresh tomatoes

1/2 cup of water

2 cups of shredded kale

A pinch of crushed red pepper

1 cup of oil cured black olives

2 teaspoons of fresh oregano plus extra

1 teaspoon of orange zest

1/4 teaspoon of black pepper

1/8 teaspoon of salt

Directions:

1. In a large pan, heat oil on medium heat and sauté the onion, garlic and fennel for 8 minutes.

2. Add ¼ teaspoon each of salt and pepper.

3. Stir in the fresh tomatoes, diced tomatoes, kale and water. Cook for 12 minutes then stir in the olives, oregano, and crushed red pepper.

4. Season the fish with orange zest, salt and pepper.

5. Nestle the cod into the tomato mixture, cover and cook for 10 minutes.

6. Garnish with extra oregano and orange zest.

7. Top with a drizzle of olive oil.

Nutrition per serving:

Calories: 257, fat: 13g, carbohydrates: 12g, proteins: 23g

Greek Grain Salad

Enjoy this with the extra crunchiness of pita chips.

Servings: 6-8

Prep time: 15 minutes

Cook time: 30 minutes

Ingredients:

2 cups of water

1 cup of mixed quinoa, buckwheat and millet

Salt

For the salad:

½ pound of feta, crumbled

1 (14 oz) can black olives, drained, sliced

3 vine ripe tomatoes, seeded, chopped

2 small seedless cucumbers, diced

1 red onion, diced

3 bell peppers (red, yellow and green), seeded, diced

For the dressing:

6 tablespoons of red wine vinegar

½ cup of olive oil

1 teaspoon of dried oregano

For the pita chips:

12 ounces of mini pitas, quartered

Sea salt, to taste

Olive oil, to taste

Directions:

1. In a medium pot, add the grains and a little sprinkling of salt. Pour in water and allow to come to a boil.

2. Reduce heat, cover and simmer for 15-20 minutes.

3. Turn off the heat, allow to sit for 5 minutes, still covered. Use a fork to fluff.

4. Toss all the salad ingredients together in a large bowl then add the grains to the salad.

5. Whisk the dressing ingredients together; drizzle over the salad/grain mixture and toss together.

6. Heat oven to 375°F and line a baking pan with parchment paper.

7. Arrange the pitas evenly on the pan; brush with oil and season with salt.

8. Bake for 12-15 minutes or until crisp.

Nutrition per serving:

Calories: 525, fat: 32.9g, carbohydrates: 48.2g, proteins: 12.9g

Pasta Salad

Servings: 6-8

Prep time: 15 minutes

Cook time: 5 minutes

Ingredients:

1/2 pound whole wheat pasta

1/3 cup radish, finely diced

2 bell peppers (orange and yellow), diced finely

1/3 cup cucumber, finely diced

1 small red onion, diced finely

1/3 cup tomato, finely diced, excess liquid drained

1/3 cup diced pepperoncini

1/3 cup black olives, diced finely

1/3 cup green olives, halved

1 handful fresh thyme leaves

1 teaspoon of dried oregano

Salt

Fresh cracked black pepper

1/4 cup of olive oil plus extra

1 lemon, juiced

1/3 cup feta cheese, finely diced

Directions:

1. Add water and some salt to a pot and bring to a boil. Add the pasta and cook until al dente. Drain the pasta thoroughly and rinse with cold water.

2. Add the pasta to a bowl and toss with oil to prevent it from sticking together.

3. Add the oregano, vegetables olives, salt, pepper and thyme.

4. Pour in the lemon juice and oil; toss to combine.

5. Fold the cheese into the salad.

6. Chill for 2 hours in the refrigerator or overnight.

7. Adjust seasoning if needed.

8. Garnish with fresh thyme and serve.

Nutrition per serving:

Calories: 244, fat: 13.6g, carbohydrates: 26.3g, proteins: 6.2g

Mediterranean Farro Salad

Servings: 4-6

Prep time: 10 minutes

Cook time: 40 minutes

Ingredients:

For the salad:

1 ½ cups of pearled farro

2 ½ cups of low-sodium vegetable broth

1 ¼ cups of water

2 cups of baby spinach leaves, roughly chopped

1 can of chickpeas, drained, rinsed

1 cucumber, peeled and chopped

2 cups cherry tomatoes, halved

½ small red onion, thinly sliced

1 small green pepper, chopped

¾ cup of crumbled feta

1 tablespoon olive oil

For dressing:

¼ cup of olive oil

2 tablespoons lemon juice, freshly squeezed

1 tablespoon of honey

1 tablespoon of red wine vinegar

¼ teaspoon of salt

¼ teaspoon of oregano

1 pinch of red pepper flakes

Directions:

1. In a medium saucepan, heat oil on medium heat and cook the farro for 1 minute with frequent stirring.

2. Pour in the broth and water; increase the heat and allow to come to a boil.

3. Cover the pan, turn down heat to medium low and simmer for about 30-35 minutes or until the farro is softened and a bit chewy. Drain any extra liquid and scoop into a large bowl.

4. Add the spinach and toss to mix; the spinach will wilt slightly from the heat. Leave to cool for 15-20 minutes.

5. Add the cucumber, tomatoes, chickpeas, red onion, pepper and feta cheese; toss together to mix.

6. Whisk all the dressing ingredients, minus the olive oil, in a small bowl. Stir in the oil and thoroughly whisk until smooth.

7. Add some of the dressing to the farro; toss together to mix. Taste and keep adding dressing until it gets to your desired taste.

10. Adjust seasoning if necessary.

Nutrition per serving:

Calories: 626, fat: 20.2g, carbohydrates: 88.4g, proteins: 27.8g

Tuna Salad With Avocado And Yogurt Dressing

These ingredients blend nicely to create a creamy tuna salad.

Servings: 4

Preparation time: 10 minutes

Cooking time: 0 minute

Ingredients:

2 (4-oz) cans of tuna fish

1/4 cup of plain Greek yogurt

1 ripe avocado

1/2 teaspoon of onion powder

1/2 teaspoon garlic powder

1 tablespoon of dill relish

1 tablespoon lemon juice

1 celery stalk, finely chopped

1/2 red onion, diced finely

Salt, to taste

Black ground pepper, to taste

Directions:

1. Combine the yoghurt and avocado in a medium-sized bowl then mash until you have a smooth paste.
2. Stir in the onion powder, garlic powder, dill relish, salt and pepper. Mix thoroughly.
1. Add fish, celery and red onion then gently stir to coat evenly.
3. Add the lemon juice and stir.

Nutrition per serving:

Calories: 175, fat: 11g, carbohydrates: 11g, proteins: 11.5g

Tzatziki Turkey Meatballs

These delicious meatballs are topped with yummy in tzatziki sauce.

Servings: 4

Prep time: 10 minutes

Cook time: 16 minutes

Ingredients:

4 whole wheat flatbreads

1 cup of diced cucumber

1 cup of diced tomato

1/2 cup of thinly sliced red onion

For the meatballs:

1 pound of ground turkey

1 cup chopped fresh spinach

1/4 cup of finely diced red onion

1 teaspoon oregano

2 garlic cloves, minced

Pepper

Salt

2 tablespoons olive oil

For the tzatziki sauce:

1/2 cup of plain greek yogurt

2 tablespoons of lemon juice

1/4 cup of grated cucumber

1/2 teaspoon of garlic powder

1/2 teaspoon of dry dill

Salt

Directions:

1. Add all the meatball ingredients to a large bowl except olive oil.

2. Combine the ingredients with your hands until the mixture sticks together and can be shaped into balls. Form into balls of 1-inch diameter. You should get up to 12 meatballs.

2. Heat a large pan on medium high heat and add the oil.

4. Cook the meatballs for about 3-4 minutes per side until it is browned all over. Transfer to a platter and set aside.

5. Meanwhile, combine the tzatziki ingredients in a small bowl until well mixed.

6. To serve, add 3 meatballs on a flatbread, follow the meatballs with the cucumber, onion and tomato.

7. Add the tzatziki sauce as topping.

Nutrition per serving:

Calories: 429, fat: 19g, carbohydrates: 38g, proteins: 28g

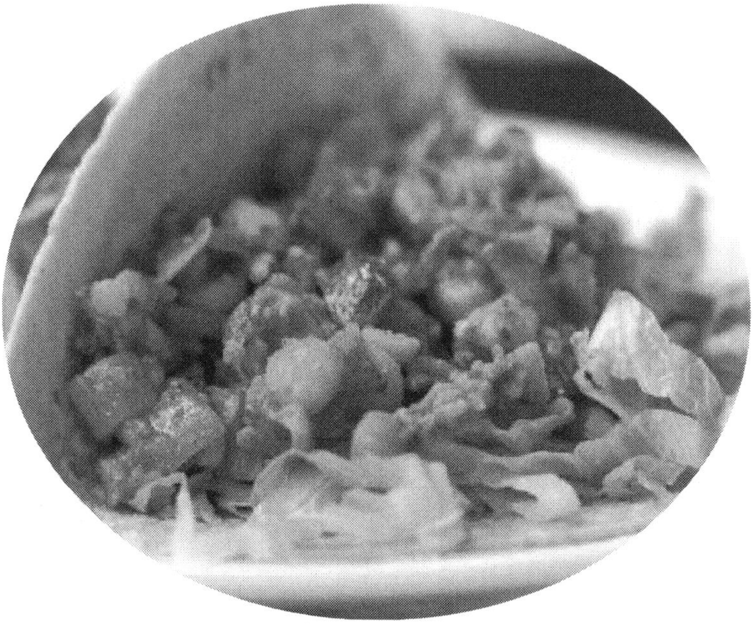

Greek Tacos With Vegetable Dressing

Servings: 4

Prep time: 10 minutes

Cook time: 0 minutes

Ingredients:

8 flour tortillas

1 cup of feta cheese, crumbled

1 cup cucumber and dill dips

For the salad:

4 cups of romaine lettuce, shredded

2 cups of grilled chicken

1 cup of diced tomatoes

1/2 cup of Greek dressing

1/2 cup of black olives, sliced

1/4 cup of diced cilantro

3/4 cup of diced cucumbers

Directions:

1. In a bowl, toss all the salad ingredients together excluding the feta.

2. Scoop the salad onto the tortillas.

3. Sprinkle with the feta then drizzle the dip over it.

Nutrition per serving:

Calories: 347, fat: 13.5g, carbohydrates: 28.2g, proteins: 29.3g

Chicken Pasta Salad

This is good eaten at room temperature or chilled.

Servings: 4

Prep time: 15 minutes

Cook time: 0 minutes

Ingredients:

1 (12 oz) package of cooked whole wheat pasta, drained

1 1/4 cup of Greek salad dressing

1/2 cup of balsamic vinegar

1 (2.25 oz) can of sliced black olives, optional

1/2 cup of finely diced green onions

2 cups of shredded cooked chicken

1 teaspoon of garlic powder

2 tablespoons of dill weed

2 (4oz) packages of feta cheese

1 cup sliced cherry tomatoes

Directions:

1. Combine the pasta with vinegar and Greek dressing.

2. Add the olives, green onions and chicken then mix thoroughly.

3. Stir in the dill weed and garlic powder.

4. Add the tomatoes and cheese; toss lightly.

5. Keep it the fridge for at least 3 hours to absorb the liquid and blend the flavors.

Nutrition per serving:

Calories: 524, fat: 16.3g, carbohydrates: 53.2g, proteins: 38.7g

Crockpot Mediterranean Chicken

This chicken is juicy and really tasty.

Servings: 4

Prep time: 5 minutes

Cook time: 4 hours

Ingredients:

4 chicken breasts, boneless and skinless

1 cup of kalamata olives

1 medium onion, chopped

2 tablespoons of capers

1 cup of roasted red peppers, roughly chopped

1 medium lemon, juiced

1 tablespoon of minced garlic

3 teaspoons of Italian seasoning

Pepper

Salt

Fresh thyme, optional

Directions:

1. Rub the chicken all over with salt and pepper.

2. In a large pan, brown the chicken for 1-2 minutes per side on medium high heat.

3. Coat a slow cooker with cooking spray and add the browned chicken.

4. Add the olives, capers, onions and red pepper to the sides of the cooker; don't let them cover the chicken.

5. In a small bowl, whisk together the garlic, Italian seasoning and lemon juice. Pour this mixture over the chicken.

6. Cover cooker and cook for 2 hours on high or 4 hours on low.

7. Garnish with thyme if you like.

Nutrition per serving:

Calories: 174, fat: 6.2g, carbohydrates: 7.1g, proteins: 22.2g

Flatbread Pizza

Servings: 3

Prep time: 15 minutes

Cook time: 10 minutes

Ingredients:

3 pieces naan or pita bread

1/2 cup of marinated artichoke hearts, chopped

1/2 medium avocado, thinly sliced

1/2 cup of cherry tomatoes, halved

1/4 small red onion, thinly sliced

2 ounces of crumbled feta cheese with herbs

Fine sea salt

For the pesto:

2 cups of packed baby spinach

1/4 cup of fresh basil leaves, torn

1/4 cup of almonds

2/3 cup of cannellini beans, drained, rinsed

1 tablespoon of extra-virgin olive oil

2 tablespoons of water

1/8 teaspoon of pepper

1/4 teaspoon of fine sea salt

Directions:

1. Preheat oven to 350°F.

2. Arrange the bread on a baking pan.

3. Pulse all the pesto ingredients in a food processor until smooth. Scoop a spoonful of the pesto on each pita bread.

4. Arrange the artichoke hearts, tomatoes, red onion and avocados on the spread, top with a sprinkling of feta then season with sea salt.

6. Bake for 10 minutes or until the bread becomes lightly crispy.

7. Let cool for a bit before slicing with a pizza cutter.

Nutrition per serving:

Cal: 450, fat: 19g, carbohydrates: 57g, proteins: 17g

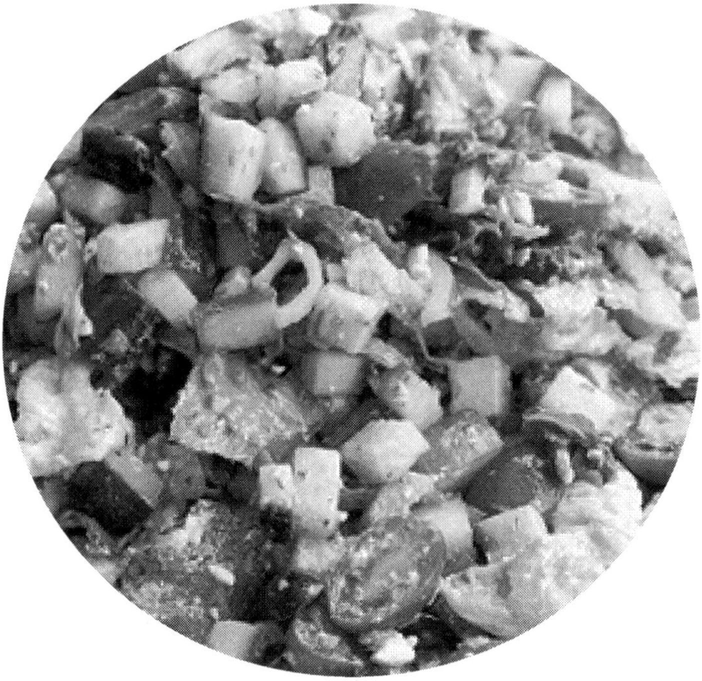

Chopped Lunch Salad

This colorful variety of nutrients is good for your body.

Servings: 4

Prep time: 10 minutes

Cook time: 0 minutes

Ingredients:

For the dressing:

1/4 cup plus 2 tablespoons of extra-virgin olive oil

1/4 cup of lemon juice

Himalayan pink salt

For the salad:

1/2 cup of Persian cucumber, chopped

1/2 cup of hearts of palm, chopped

1/2 cup of artichoke hearts, chopped

1/2 cup of tomatoes, chopped

1/2 avocado, chopped

2 tablespoons of red onion, chopped

2 tablespoons of kalamata olives, chopped

1 tablespoon of capers, chopped

1 teaspoon of fresh basil, chopped

Directions:

1. Pulse all the dressing ingredients in a blender until well blended; taste and adjust seasoning.

2. Combine the salad ingredients together.

3. Drizzle the dressing over the salad and toss to coat.

Nutrition per serving:

Calories: 132, fat: 13.2g, carbohydrates: 4.2g, proteins: 0.8g

Fish Tacos

Servings: 4

Prep time: 10 minutes

Cook time: 10 minutes

Ingredients:

8 small corn tortillas

1 pound of firm white fish

Pepper

Salt

1 tablespoon olive oil

2 cups of shredded cabbage

1 cup of kalamata olives, halved

1 cup of grape or cherry tomatoes, thinly sliced

1 cucumber, seeded, diced

Tzatziki sauce

1/2 cup of crumbled feta cheese

Directions:

1. Season the fish on both sides generously with pepper and salt.

2. In a large pan, heat oil on medium high heat and cook the fish for about 3-4 minutes on each side until fish is opaque, easily flakes and is well cooked. Transfer to a plate.

3. Flake the fish into small pieces with two forks.

4. To make the tacos, layer the ingredients in the following order: begin with the cabbage, fish pieces, sliced tomatoes, halved olives, and end with the cucumber.

5. Top with the cheese and tzatziki.

Nutrition per serving:

Calories: 306, fat: 13.9g, carbohydrates: 30.8g, proteins: 17.2gs

Souvlaki Bowl With Salmon

This is a twist on the classic Greek street food.

Servings: 4

Prep time: 15 minutes

Cook time: 5 minutes

Ingredients:

For the souvlaki:

1 pound of fresh salmon, cut into 4 parts

2 garlic cloves, grated

6 tablespoons of lemon juice

2 tablespoons of balsamic vinegar

3 tablespoons of olive oil

1 tablespoon of paprika

1 tablespoon of fresh oregano

1 tablespoon of fresh dill

1 teaspoon of pepper

1/2 teaspoon of salt

For the bowl:

1 cup of dry pearl couscous

2 tablespoons of olive oil

1 inch zucchini cut into 1/4 rounds

2 red peppers, quartered

6 ounces of feta cheese crumbled

1 cup of cherry tomatoes halved

1/2 cup of kalamata olives

2 Persian cucumbers sliced

Directions:

1. Mix all the souvlaki ingredients, excluding the salmon, in a medium bowl. Toss with the salmon to completely coat. Allow to stand for 10-15 minutes.

2. In the meantime, cook the couscous according to instructions on the package.

3. Toss the 2 teaspoon oil, zucchini, red pepper, salt and pepper together in a bowl.

4. Preheat a grill to medium high.

5. Place the salmon on the grill and cook for about 3 minutes per side or until salmon is well cooked. Remove from the grill.

6. While grilling the salmon, also grill the zucchini and bell peppers for 3-4 minutes on each side or until you see char marks. Remove the salmon and veggies from grill.

7. Evenly divide the couscous among 4 bowls and drizzle lemon juice over each portion.

8. Top with the grilled vegetables, tomatoes, salmon, cucumbers, cheese and olives.

9. Add a little tzatziki on top and serve with a garnish of herbs.

Nutrition per serving:

Calories: 612, fat: 33.2g, carbohydrates: 47.8g, proteins: 34g

White Bean Salad

It's very simple and quick.

Servings: 10

Prep time: 5 minutes

Cook time: 0 minutes

Ingredients:

6 (15-oz) cans of cannellini beans

1 1/2 ounces of red wine vinegar

1 cup of pesto

5 celery stalks, sliced

4 teaspoons of kosher salt

1 medium red bell pepper, minced

1 teaspoon of black pepper

Directions:

1. Drain the beans, add to a colander and rinse with cold water then set it aside to drain

2. Toss the remaining ingredients together in a large bowl.

3. Add the beans, toss to combine and it's ready.

Nutrition per serving:

Calories: 964, fat: 12.6g, carbohydrates: 156.6g, proteins: 62.2g

Slow Cooker Chicken With Tomatoes And Artichokes

Just dump the ingredients in the pot and let the slow cooker do its job.

Servings: 6

Prep time: 5 minutes

Cook time: 5 hours

Ingredients:

4 - 6 chicken thighs, boneless

Salt

Fresh ground pepper

1 (3.5-oz) bag of julienne cut sun-dried tomatoes

1 (14.75-oz) jar of grilled artichoke hearts

1/3 cup of artichoke hearts liquid

4 garlic cloves, minced

3 tablespoons chopped fresh parsley

1/2 tablespoon of dried oregano

Directions:

1. Drain the artichoke hearts but reserve 1/3 cup of the liquid.

2. Coat a medium size slow cooker with nonstick cooking spray.

3. Use the oregano, salt and pepper to season the chicken. Place the chicken in the coated slow cooker in an even layer.

3. Top the chicken with the tomatoes, artichoke hearts and garlic then pour in the reserved liquid from the artichoke hearts.

4. Cover the cooker and cook for about 6 hours on low or 4 to 4 ½ hours on high.

5. Serve in plates and garnish with parsley.

Nutrition per serving:

Calories: 169, fat: 12g, carbohydrates: 1g, proteins: 12g

Eggplant Stuffed With Quinoa

This dish gives you a burst of well blended flavors.

Servings: 2

Prep time: 5 minutes

Cook time: 30 minutes

Ingredients:

1 eggplant, halved along the length

2 tablespoons olive oil, divided

1 cup of button mushrooms, chopped

1 medium shallot diced

1/2 cup of cooked quinoa

5 plum tomatoes, chopped

1 tablespoon of canned tomato juice

2 garlic cloves, minced

1/2 teaspoon ground cumin

1 tablespoon chopped fresh parsley plus extra

1 tablespoon tahini

1 teaspoon lemon juice

1/2 teaspoon garlic powder

Salt

Water

Pepper

Directions:

1. Preheat oven to 425°F.

2. Scoop out some flesh from the cut eggplant.

3. Set the eggplant on a baking pan and drizzle a tablespoon of oil over it.

4. Season with a sprinkling of salt then bake in the oven for 20 minutes.

5. Meanwhile, in a large pan, heat the remaining oil and sauté the mushrooms and shallots for about 5 minutes until mushrooms are tender.

7. Stir in the quinoa, minced garlic, cumin, parsley, tomatoes and tomato juice; allow to cook until the liquid is absorbed.

8. Once timer for the eggplant goes off, lower oven heat to 350°F then stuff the eggplant halves with the quinoa mix.

9. Bake for an additional 10 minutes.

10. When it's time to serve, whisk the lemon, tahini, a little water, garlic powder, a pinch of pepper and salt together. Drizzle this mixture over the eggplants.

11. Garnish with parsley.

Nutrition per serving:

Calories: 345, fat: 19g, carbohydrates: 38g, proteins: 9g

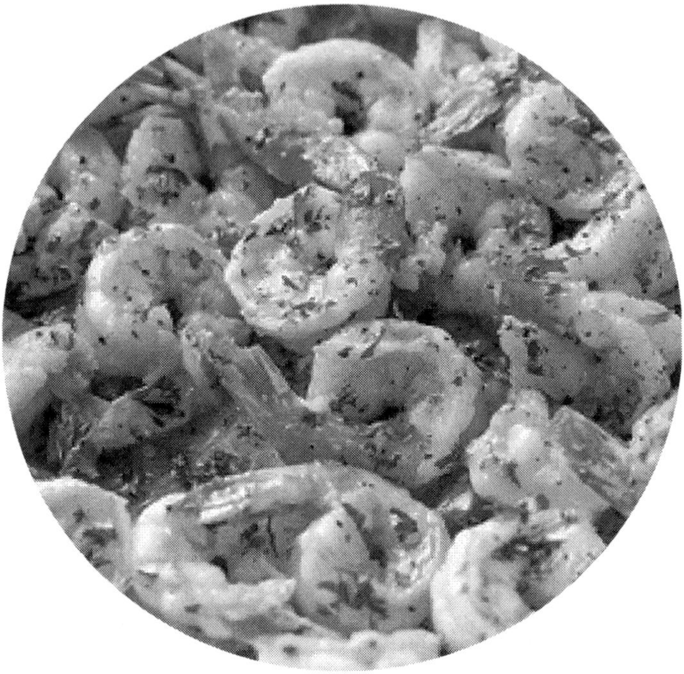

Garlic Shrimp

Servings: 4

Prep time: 10 minutes

Cook time: 5 minutes

Ingredients:

1 pound of large shrimp, peeled, deveined

1/3 cup of olive oil

¼ teaspoon of chili flakes

4 garlic cloves, finely chopped

1 teaspoon of sweet paprika

¼ teaspoon of kosher salt

1/8 teaspoon of pepper

1 ½ tablespoons of fresh lemon juice

2 tablespoons of dry sherry

2 tablespoons of chopped parsley

Directions:

1. In a large pan, add oil along with the chili flakes and garlic.

2. Increase heat to medium high and cook until garlic is aromatic and oil is hot.

3. Add the shrimp; season with pepper, paprika and salt.

4. Cook for about 2 minutes until shrimp is pink; stir frequently.

5. Pour in the lemon juice and sherry; cook for about 2-3 minutes or until shrimp is well cooked and liquid has reduced.

6. Garnish with parsley.

Nutrition per serving:

Calories: 250, fat: 17.9g, carbohydrates: 3.4g, proteins: 15.8g

Orzo Lemon Chicken Soup

Servings: 2

Prep time: 10 minutes

Cook time: 0 minutes

Ingredients:

1/2 cup of cooked whole wheat orzo

1/2 cup of roast chicken, shredded

1/2 cup of roasted zucchini pieces

3 tablespoons chopped basil, thinly sliced, divided

2 tablespoons chopped dill

1 tablespoon lemon juice

1 tablespoon of grated parmesan, optional

Black pepper

Salt

Directions:

1. In a jar, layer the orzo pasta, zucchini, meat, chopped dill and 2 tablespoons basil.

2. Drizzle with lemon juice.

3. When it's time to serve, pour boiling water into jar and fill to the top.

4. Carefully stir, cover the jar and allow to stand for 2 minutes.

5. Add salt and pepper to your taste then garnish with parmesan and basil.

Nutrition per serving:

Calories: 239, fat: 3.5g, carbohydrates: 35.5g, proteins: 16.1g

Julienned Zucchini With Garlic Shrimp

Give pasta a break with this delicious combination.

Servings: 4

Prep time: 10 minutes

Cook time: 10 minutes

Ingredients:

5 medium-sized zucchini

1 tablespoon of olive oil

5 fresh basil leaves, finely chopped

6 garlic cloves, minced

8 ounces of raw medium-sized shrimp, peeled, deveined

1/4 cup of prepared pesto

4 fresh Italian parsley, finely chopped

Sea salt, to taste

Ground black pepper, to taste

Directions:

1. Julienne the zucchinis with a vegetable peeler or use a spiralizer if you have one.

2. Add water to a large saucepan and bring to a boil on medium-high heat. Dump the zucchini into the water. Cook for 2-3 minutes or until just softened then remove from the water.

3. Add the oil to a large skillet and heat on medium-high heat.

4. Add the garlic and shrimp to the hot oil. Cook for 2-3 minutes, stirring frequently until the shrimps are firm and opaque.

5. Add the prepared pesto and cook for 1-2 minutes, stirring frequently until well-heated.

6. Add the basil and parsley then toss with the other ingredients until coated.

7. Add salt and pepper as required.

Nutrition per serving:

Calories: 250, fat: 10g, carbohydrates: 24g, proteins: 13g

Tuna And Beans

This is a wholesome delight.

Servings: 4

Prep time: 5 minutes

Cook time: 0 minutes

Ingredients:

For the dressing:

3 tablespoons of red wine vinegar

3 tablespoons of olive oil

1 teaspoon of dijon mustard

Freshly ground black pepper

Kosher salt

For the salad:

1 (7-oz) can Italian tuna packed in olive oil, drained

1 spring onion, thinly sliced

1/2 cup of canned lima beans, rinsed

1 1/4 cups of canned cannellini beans, rinsed

1 cup of grape tomatoes, quartered lengthwise

1/4 cup of basil, roughly chopped

1/4 cup of parsley, roughly chopped

1/4 cup of kalamata olives, halved

Directions:

1. Whisk the dressing ingredients in a large bowl.
2. Using a fork, crumble the tuna lightly and add to the bowl.

3. Add the rest of the ingredients.

4. Toss to coat.

5. Taste and adjust seasoning as desired.

Nutrition per serving:

Calories: 301, fat: 16g, carbohydrates: 6g, proteins: 19g

Barley Chicken Salad

Servings: 4

Prep time: 15 minutes

Cook time: 15 minutes

Ingredients:

For the barley:

1 1/2 cups of water

1/2 cup of barley

1/8 teaspoon of salt

For the salad:

5 sundried tomatoes, rehydrated, minced finely

3 mini cucumbers, diced

2 cooked chicken breasts, skinless, boneless, shredded

2 tomatoes, seeded, diced

3 tablespoons of reduced fat feta cheese, crumbled

3 tablespoons of sunflower seeds

2 tablespoons of chopped fresh tarragon

2 tablespoons of olive oil

1/2 lemon, juiced

1 tablespoon of lemon zest

1/2 teaspoon of red pepper flakes

1/2 teaspoon of sumac

Salt

Directions:

1. In a small pot, add together the barley, water and salt then bring to a boil.

2. Lower the heat to medium low and allow to simmer for about 15 minutes or until the water has been absorbed.

3. Turn off heat and leave to cool.

4. Mix the cooled barley with the remaining ingredients and serve.

Nutrition per serving:

Calories: 259, fat: 10.5g, carbohydrates: 6g, proteins: 23g

DINNER

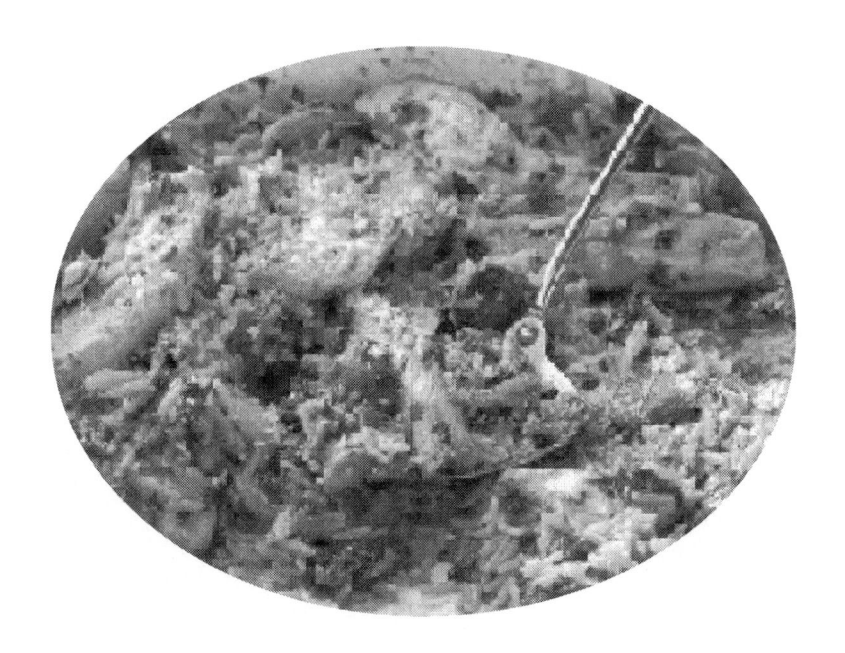

Slow Cooked Chicken And Orzo

Servings: 4

Prep time: 10 minutes

Cook time: 2 hours

Ingredients:

1 pound of chicken breasts, boneless, skinless, cut into bite size

2 medium tomatoes, chopped

1 cup of low-sodium chicken broth

1 medium onion, sliced

1 teaspoon of herbes de Provence

Juice and zest of 1 lemon

½ teaspoon of ground pepper

½ teaspoon of salt

1/3 cup of black or green olives, quartered

¾ cup of whole-wheat orzo

2 tablespoons of chopped fresh parsley

Directions:

1. In a 6-quart slow cooker, mix the chicken, broth, onion, lemon juice, herbes de Provence, tomatoes, lemon zest, pepper and salt together.

2. Cover and cook for 4 hours on low or for 2 hours on high.

3. Add the olives and orzo. Stir, cover and cook for an additional 30 minutes. Allow to cool for a few minutes.

4. Garnish with a sprinkling of parsley.

Nutrition per serving:

Calories: 278, fat: 5g, carbohydrates: 29g, proteins: 29g

Mediterranean Chicken

This is great with pasta or rice.

Servings: 4

Prep time: 20 minutes

Cook time: 1 hour

Ingredients:

8 chicken thighs, bone-in, skin-on

1 red onion, cut into 8 wedges

8 garlic cloves minced

1 cup of firm whole grape tomatoes

1 red bell pepper seeded, chopped roughly

1 orange, sliced thickly

1 lemon, sliced thickly

1 cup of Kalamata olives, pitted

3 tablespoons of capers

3 fresh rosemary springs

Juice and zest of 1 large lemon

Juice and zest of 1 large orange

1/4 cup of honey

1/3 cup of olive oil

1 tablespoon of garlic powder

1 tablespoon of onion powder

Salt

Pepper

Directions:

1. Preheat oven to 350°F.

2. In a large bowl, whisk together the orange zest, orange juice, lemon juice, lemon zest, olive oil, honey, onion powder and garlic powder. Season with a little salt.

3. Grease a large sheet pan lightly with olive oil and set aside.

4. Pat the chicken dry with paper towels. Rub all over with salt and pepper.

5. Dip each thigh into the orange mixture entirely, shake off the excess and arrange on the pan.

6. Arrange the onion, garlic, grape tomatoes, bell pepper, orange slices, and lemon slices on the pan.

7. Add the capers and olives on top.

8. Spoon the remaining orange mixture all over the chicken.

9. Add the rosemary on top.

10. Use foil to cover pan then bake for 30 minutes.

11. Remove and discard the foil then cook for an additional 40 minutes or until chicken is well cooked and golden brown.

12. Discard the rosemary and drain some of the liquid in the pan. Serve.

Nutrition per serving:

Calories: 432, fat: 30g, carbohydrates: 21g, proteins: 20g

One Pot Chicken And Lentils

Servings: 4

Prep time: 15 minutes

Cook time: 45 minutes

Ingredients:

2 pounds of chicken thighs, bone-in and skin-on

1/4 teaspoon of pepper

1/2 teaspoon of salt

1 tablespoon of olive oil

2 garlic cloves, sliced thinly

1 onion, chopped finely

1 teaspoon of smoked paprika

1 teaspoon of dried oregano

1 teaspoon of ground coriander

1 cup oil-packed sliced roasted red peppers

2 cups of low-sodium chicken stock

2 cups of canned whole tomatoes with juice

1 cup of split red lentils

1/2 cup of crumbled feta cheese

1/2 cup of sliced black olives

2 tablespoons of fresh parsley or oregano, finely chopped

Directions:

1. Preheat oven to 400°F.

2. Heat the oil in a 12-inch oven-safe pan over medium high heat.

3. Use paper towel to pat both sides of the chicken dry; generously season with pepper and salt.

4. Cook the chicken in the pan for 4 minutes per side until golden brown then transfer to a plate and cover with foil.

5. Leave about 1 tablespoon of oil in the pan and drain the rest.

6. Reduce heat to medium heat and sauté the garlic, onion, oregano, paprika and coriander for about 5 minutes or until onions are translucent.

7. Add the peppers, stock, tomatoes and lentils. Use the back of a wooden spoon to crush the tomatoes and stir everything together.

8. Nestle the chicken on the mixture, along with its juices left on the plate.

9. Bake in the oven, uncovered, for 25-30 minutes.

10. When done, add more seasoning if needed.

11. Top with feta, olives and fresh herbs.

Nutrition per serving:

Calories: 480, fat: 14g, carbohydrates: 57g, proteins: 33g

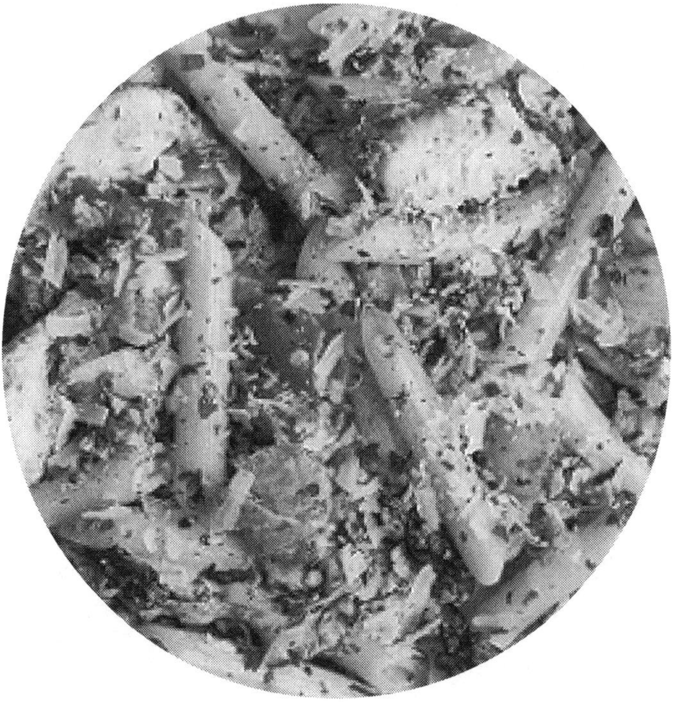

One Pot Chicken Penne

Servings: 4-5

Prep time: 10 minutes

Cook time: 15 minutes

Ingredients:

½ pound whole grain penne pasta

2 large chicken breasts, cut into bite size pieces

1/4 cup of extra virgin olive oil

4 garlic cloves, minced

3/4 cup of water

2 cups of chicken broth

1 (15-oz) can of quartered artichoke hearts, chopped roughly

A pinch of red chili pepper flakes

1 cup of cherry tomatoes, halved

2 tablespoons of drained capers

2 tablespoons of fresh lemon juice

1 cup of freshly grated parmesan cheese

1/2 cup of lightly packed fresh basil leaves, chopped

Salt

Pepper

Directions:

1. In a large pan, heat oil over medium high heat.

2. Sprinkle salt and pepper on the chicken pieces and toss to coat. Cook for 2-3 minutes in the pan until golden brown.

3. Add the garlic to the pan; cook and stir for an extra 30 seconds.

4. Stir in the water, broth, artichoke hearts, pepper flakes, pepper and ½ teaspoon of salt then allow the mixture to come to a boil.

5. Add the pasta and submerge in the liquid; cover the pan and reduce the heat to medium.

6. Simmer for about 2 minutes less than the instructions on package.

7. Add tomatoes, lemon juice and capers; increase heat to high and cook for 2-3 minutes until the sauce reduces.

8. Turn off heat; stir in the basil and cheese; allow to rest for 2-3 minutes so it can thicken before you serve.

Nutrition per serving:

Calories: 431, fat: 17.7g, carbohydrates: 44.9g, proteins: 25.7g

Easy Mediterranean Pasta

With this recipe, there is very little washing up to do.

Servings: 4

Prep time: 10 minutes

Cook time: 15 minutes

Ingredients:

8 ounces of whole wheat spaghetti noodles

1 tablespoon of extra virgin olive oil

5 garlic cloves

1 cup of red onion chopped

1/4 teaspoon of dried oregano

1 (14.5-oz) can of low sodium diced tomatoes

1 1/2 cups of low sodium chicken stock

3 cups of fresh spinach

1 cup of garbanzo beans

1/3 cup of kalamata olives

1/2 cup of feta cheese, divided

1/2 teaspoon of salt

Directions:

1. In a large pot, heat oil over medium high heat then sauté the onion and garlic until onion turns translucent and garlic starts to brown.

2. Stir in the stock, oregano and diced tomatoes.

3. Submerged the noodles in the liquid and allow to come to a boil.

4. Lower the heat to medium low; cook for 6-8 minutes.

5. Reduce heat again to low and stir; season with salt.

6. Stir in the spinach slowly, adding it a cup at a time.

7. Stir in the olives, garbanzo beans and ¼ cup of cheese.

8. Serve and garnish with the remaining cheese.

Nutrition per serving:

Calories: 487, fat: 13.8g, carbohydrates: 70.5g, proteins: 22.5g

Chicken And Vegetables

You can top this with feta cheese and kalamata olives.

Servings: 6

Prep time: 10 minutes

Cook time: 25 minutes

Ingredients:

1 pound of baby potatoes, cubed

1 1/2 pounds of chicken breast, boneless, skinless, cubed

2 tablespoons of avocado oil

2 bell peppers, cut into chunks

1/2 yellow onion, cut into chunks

1 tablespoon of Mediterranean seasoning

Directions:

1. Preheat your oven to 400°F.

2. Place parchment paper on a baking pan.

3. Combine all the ingredients in the baking pan then toss to coat with the oil and seasoning.

4. Bake for 20-25 minutes or until chicken is well cooked.

Nutrition per serving:

Calories: 296, fat: 13g, carbohydrates: 18g, proteins: 25g

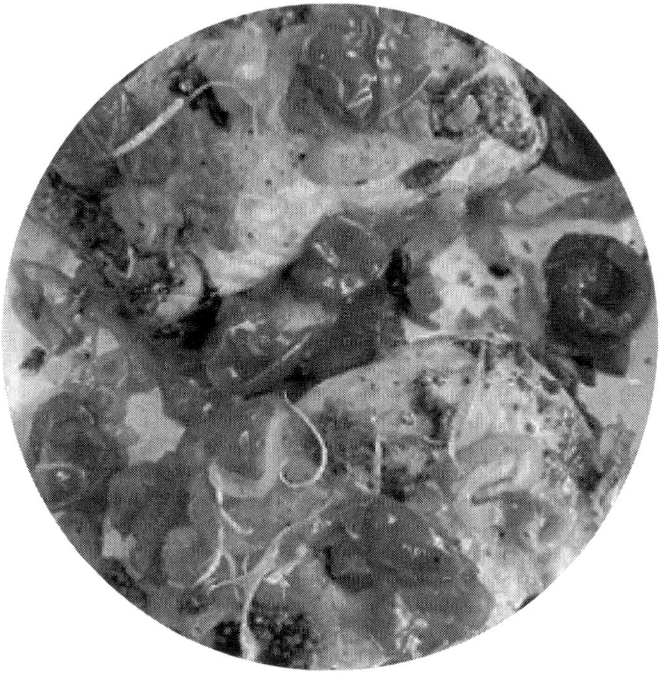

Salmon And Tomatoes

Servings: 6

Prep time: 10 minutes

Cook time: 20 minutes

Ingredients:

1 large whole salmon filet

2 cups of cherry tomatoes, halved

Some marinated sweet or hot peppers

1/2 cup of assorted olives, pitted

2 small lemons, sliced thinly

1/4 red onion, sliced thinly

4 tablespoons of extra virgin olive oil

2 teaspoons of capers

Kosher salt

Freshly cracked pepper

Chopped fresh parsley

Directions:

1. Preheat your oven to 425°F.

2. Place parchment paper on a baking pan.

3. Set the filet on the pan then arrange the slices of lemon, onions, olives, capers, tomato, and peppers around the filet and on top.

4. Drizzle oil over the arrangement and season with salt and pepper.

5. Bake for about 20-30 minutes or until the fish is thoroughly cooked and easily flakes with a fork.

6. Garnish with the herbs and serve.

Nutrition per serving:

Calories: 150, fat: 12.5g, carbohydrates: 5.3g, proteins: 6.6g

Mediterranean Cod
Absolutely delicious

Servings: 2

Prep time: 8 minutes

Cook time: 20 minutes

Ingredients:

1 pound of cod, cut into four pieces

1/2 cup of whole olives, pitted, halved, chopped

8 spears of asparagus

2 plum tomatoes, halved

1/2 leek, sliced and halved

1 white onion, quartered

2 tablespoons of olive oil

1/2 teaspoon of oregano

1/2 teaspoon of red pepper flakes

1/8 teaspoon black pepper

1/8 teaspoon Himalayan salt

Directions:

1. Preheat the oven to 400°F.

2. Line a large sheet pan with parchment paper.

3. Arrange the fish and the veggies on the prepared pan.

4. Drizzle with the olive oil and season with oregano, red pepper flakes, pepper and salt.

5. Bake for 20-22 minutes.

Nutrition per serving:

Calories: 274, fat: 18.6g, carbohydrates: 17.7g, proteins: 13.7g

Slow Cooked Beef Stew
This is exactly what you need for cold nights.

Servings: 10

Prep time: 5 minutes

Cook time: 8 hours

Ingredients:

3 pounds of beef stew meat

16 ounces of baby portabello or crimini mushrooms, sliced

2 cans (14.5-ounce) of diced tomatoes, drained

1 can (15-ounce) of tomato sauce

10 garlic cloves minced

1 large onion chopped

2 cups of beef broth

1/2 cup of balsamic vinegar

1 jar (2-ounce) of capers drained

1 can (6-ounce) of black olives drained

2 tablespoons of dried rosemary

Salt

Pepper

Chopped fresh parsley

Grated parmesan cheese

Directions:

1. Gently combine the meat, mushrooms, tomatoes, tomato sauce, garlic, onion, rosemary, broth, vinegar, olives, and capers in a 6-qt slow cooker.

2. Cook for 8-10 hours on low.

3. Add salt and pepper as needed.

4. Serve in bowls and garnish with parsley and parmesan.

Nutrition per serving:

Calories: 273, fat: 9g, carbohydrates: 16g, proteins: 33g

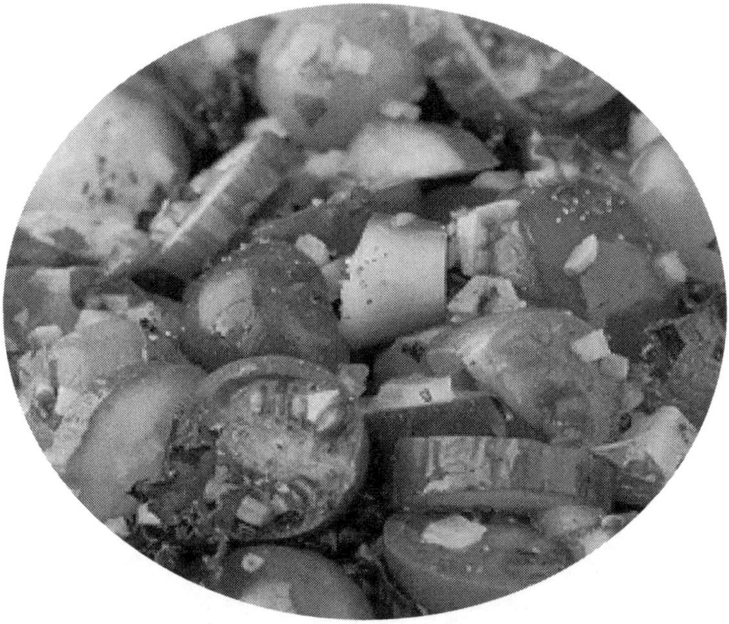

Greek Salad

This is a real classic Greek recipe.

Servings: 4

Prep time: 15 minutes

Cook time: 0 minutes

Ingredients:

For the salad:

1/2 cup of black pitted olives, halved

1/2 cup of chickpeas

2 large tomatoes, cut into 1-inch pieces

2 medium cucumbers, cubed

1 red bell pepper, cut into 1-inch pieces

1 medium red onion, sliced thinly

1/2 cup of feta cheese, cubed

For the dressing:

1/4 cup of extra virgin olive oil

2 tablespoons of red wine vinegar

1/4 cup of fresh parsley, chopped

1 teaspoon of salt

1 teaspoon of oregano

1/2 teaspoon of black pepper

Directions:

1. Add all the salad ingredients to a large bowl, excluding the feta cheese; gently toss to mix.

2. Whisk all the dressing ingredients in a small bowl and drizzle over the salad.

3. Add the cheese then gently toss to mix.

Nutrition per serving:

Calories: 273, fat: 20g, carbohydrates: 17g, proteins: 6g

Shrimp And Chickpeas Salad
This comes handy when you want a very easy dinner.

Servings: 4

Prep time: 15 minutes

Cook time: 0 minutes

Ingredients:

1 pound of cooked medium shrimp, peeled and deveined, cut in half crosswise,

1 (15.5-oz) can of chickpeas, rinsed

1/2 head of romaine lettuce, cut into thin strips crosswise

1/2 English cucumber, chopped

1/2 medium sweet onion, chopped

2 cups of pita chips, broken into pieces

1/2 cup of pitted Kalamata olives, halved

3/4 cup of crumbled feta

2 tablespoons of red wine vinegar

3 tablespoons of olive oil

¼ teaspoon of kosher salt

¼ teaspoon of black pepper

Directions:

1. Toss all the ingredients together in a large bowl.

2. Serve.

Nutrition per serving:

Calories: 766, fat: 27g, carbohydrates: 80.9g, proteins: 52.5g

Crockpot Garlic Potatoes And Chicken
Start this before going to work and return to a yummy feast.

Servings: 4

Prep time: 10 minutes

Cook time: 8 hours

Ingredients:

8 chicken thighs, bone-in, skin-on

2 pounds of baby red potatoes, quartered

1/2 teaspoon of dried oregano

1/2 teaspoon of dried basil

1/4 teaspoon of dried rosemary

Kosher salt

Freshly ground black pepper

4 tablespoons of olive oil, divided

4 garlic cloves, minced

1/2 teaspoon of dried thyme

2 tablespoons of chopped fresh parsley leaves

1 cup of freshly grated parmesan

Directions:

1. Season the meat with oregano, basil, salt, pepper and rosemary.

2. In a large pan, heat 2 tablespoons of olive oil medium high heat and sauté the seasoned chicken for about 2-3 minutes on each side until golden brown; drain any excess fat.

3. In a slow cooker, add the potatoes and combine with the garlic, thyme and reserved oil. Add salt and pepper to your preference.

4. Arrange the browned chicken in a single layer in the cooker.

5. Cook for 3-4 hours on high or 7-8 hours on low or until chicken is well cooked.

6. To serve, garnish with a sprinkling of cheese and parsley.

Nutrition per serving:

Calories: 551, fat: 26.7g, carbohydrates: 38.4g, proteins: 38.9g

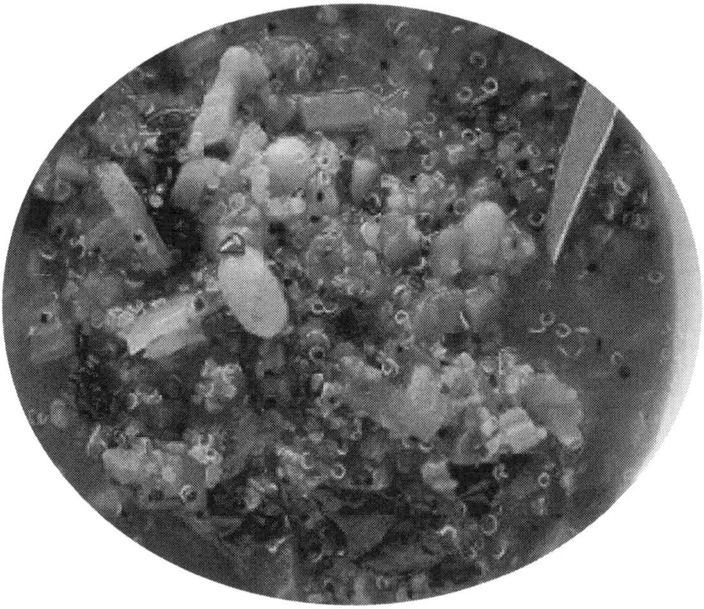

White Bean Kale Quinoa Soup

This soup is rich and nutritious.

Servings: 6

Prep time: 15 minutes

Cook time: 4 hours

Ingredients:

2 (15.5-oz) cans of cannellini beans, undrained

1 (14.5-oz) can of diced tomatoes, undrained

3/4 cup of uncooked quinoa, rinsed

4 cups chicken broth

1/2 cup of yellow onion chopped

3 garlic cloves, minced

2 teaspoons of Italian seasoning

3 cups of chopped kale

Freshly grated parmesan cheese

Salt

Pepper

Directions:

1. Add the quinoa to a crockpot and pour 2 cups of broth over it.

2. Add 1 can of the beans and diced tomatoes.

3. Add the onion, garlic and Italian seasoning; garnish with pepper and salt.

4. Pulse the remaining can of beans and broth in a food processor or blender until smooth then pour this mixture into the crockpot.

5. Stir everything thoroughly and cover.

6. Cook for 3-4 hours on high.

7. When it is 15 minutes to the end of cooking time, stir in the kale. Taste and adjust seasoning if required.

8. Ladle into bowls and garnish with parmesan cheese.

Nutrition per serving:

Calories: 607, fat: 3.5g, carbohydrates: 106.6g, proteins: 40.9g

Salmon Olives And Veggies

Servings: 4

Prep time: 10 minutes

Cook time: 8 minutes

Ingredients:

4 salmon fillets

2 tablespoons of lemon juice

1 tablespoon of parsley

1 tablespoon of basil

1 tablespoon of garlic powder

6 green olives, chopped

3 sprigs of fresh dill

1 small red onion, diced

1 large tomato, diced

1 medium English cucumber, diced

Cracked black pepper

Directions:

1. In a small bowl, mix the lemon juice, parsley, basil and garlic together.

2. Arrange the salmon in a shallow dish, spray with cooking spray then sprinkle with some black pepper.

3. Spoon the lemon juice mixture over the salmon; cover and chill for 30 minutes in the refrigerator.

4. Preheat a grill to high heat.

5. Combine the red onion, olives, dill, tomato and cucumber in a medium bowl and set aside.

6. Place the salmon on the grill with the herbed side facing down and cook for about 4 minutes or until the edges become white.

8. Carefully flip and cover with aluminum foil.

9. Reduce heat or move the salmon to cooler areas on the grill; cook for about 4 minutes or until the fish is opaque.

10. To serve, add the olive mixture on top of each salmon

Nutrition per serving:

Calories: 370.1, fat: 18.9g, carbohydrates: 3.9g, proteins: 39.3g

Easy Prawns

Servings: 4

Prep time: 5 minute

Cook time: 10 minutes

Ingredients:

1 pound of frozen raw king prawns, peeled, tails off, thawed

1 tablespoon olive oil

4 garlic cloves, sliced thinly

1 onion, diced finely

½ cup of dry white wine

2 ½ cups of tomato and garlic pasta sauce

½ cup of pitted green or Kalamata olives, halved

2 tablespoons of chopped fresh oregano

Pepper, to taste

Cooked brown rice or steamed vegetables for serving

Directions:

1. In a large pan, heat oil on medium heat and sauté the onions for about 3-4 minutes or until tender.

2. Add the garlic and continue cooking and stirring for another minute.

3. Add the wine and cook until it is reduced by half.

4. Stir in the olives and pasta sauce; allow to come to a boil then turn down heat to low.

5. Add the prawns, stir and leave to simmer for about 4-5 minutes or until well cooked.

6. Stir in the oregano and pepper.

7. Serve with cooked brown rice or steamed vegetables.

Nutrition per serving:

Calories: 210, fat: 4g, carbohydrates: 10.5g, proteins: 27.3g

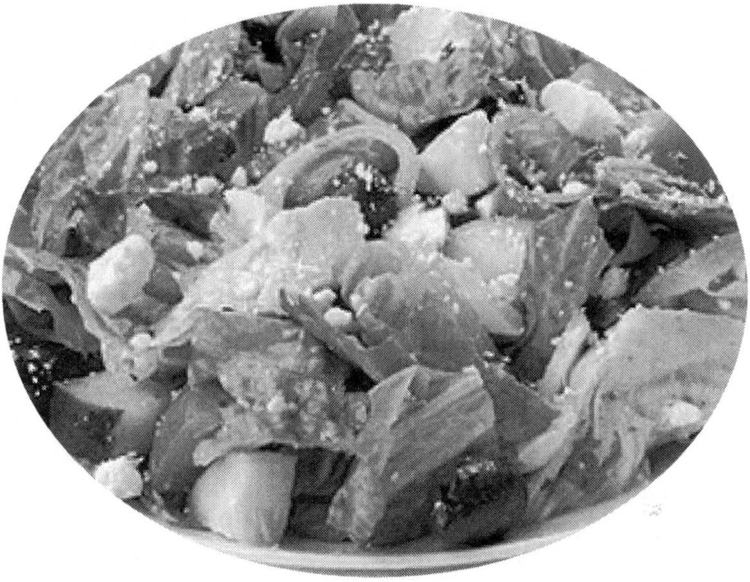

Crab Salad

This is a zesty meal for a light dinner.

Servings: 1

Prep time: 10 minutes

Cook time: 0 minutes

Ingredients:

4 ounces of mixed greens

2 ounces of fresh crab

1/4 cup of diced kalamata olives

1/4 cup of diced cucumber

6 cherry tomatoes, cut in half

1 tablespoon of extra virgin olive oil

1 tablespoon of champagne vinegar

1 tablespoon of fresh mint

Fresh ground pepper

Directions:

1. In a bowl, combine the greens, cucumbers, tomatoes, olives and crab together.

2. Drizzle the vinegar and oil over it.

3. Sprinkle with the mint and ground pepper.

Nutrition per serving:

Calories: 409, fat: 20.1g, carbohydrates: 43.6g, proteins: 21.8g

Mediterranean Quesadillas

You'll love this.

Servings: 8

Prep time: 20 minutes

Cook time: 10 minutes

Ingredients:

8 (8-inch) whole wheat tortillas

1/2 cup of chopped pitted kalamata olives

1/2 cup of julienned sun dried tomatoes in olive oil, drained

1 tablespoon of fresh dill

1 (10-ounce) package of frozen chopped spinach, thawed, drained

1 cup of crumbled feta cheese

1 cup of shredded mozzarella cheese

For the tzatziki:

1 cup of plain Greek yogurt

2 garlic cloves, crushed

1 English cucumber, diced finely

1 tablespoon freshly squeezed lemon juice

1 tablespoon of chopped fresh dill

1 teaspoon of chopped fresh mint, optional

1 teaspoon of lemon zest

2 tablespoons of olive oil

Kosher salt

Freshly ground black pepper

Directions:

1. In a small bowl, mix all the tzatziki ingredients together excluding the oil, salt and pepper. When fully mixed, add salt and pepper to taste then drizzle the oil over it. Chill for about 10 to 15 minutes in the refrigerator for the flavors to blend.

2. Preheat your oven to 400°F. Place parchment paper on a baking sheet.

3. Add 1/4 of the tomatoes, spinach, cheeses and olives on a tortilla, cover with another tortilla to make a quesadilla and place on the prepared baking pan. Repeat this process for the remaining tortillas.

4. Bake for about 8-10 minutes until cheese melts.

5. Serve with the tzatziki and garnish with dill.

Nutrition per serving:

Calories: 384.8, fat: 18.5g, carbohydrates: 32.6g, proteins: 14.4g

Tangy Chicken Dinner

This mouthwatering dinner is ready with just a few ingredients.

Servings: 12

Prep time: 30 minutes

Cook time: 15 minutes

Ingredients:

3 pounds chicken breasts

4 tablespoons of balsamic vinegar

1 teaspoon ginger

1 tablespoon red chili sauce

1 tablespoon honey

Directions:

1. Preheat your oven to 405°F.

2. Mix together balsamic vinegar, red chili sauce, honey and ginger in a small bowl.

3. Put the chicken in a Ziploc bag then pour in the balsamic mixture. Shake to coat then set aside so that it marinates for 30 minutes.

4. Transfer the chicken pieces to a sheet pan. Bake for about 15 minutes.

Nutrition per serving:

Calories: 133, fat: 2g, carbohydrates:4g, proteins: 27g

Vegetable Soup

This soup is not only pleasing to the eye, it will also keep you warm.

Servings: 14

Prep time: 14 minutes

Cook time: 18 minutes

Ingredients:

2 garlic cloves, crushed

1 small onion, chopped

4 cups of chopped cabbage

1 cup of chopped carrots

1 cup of green beans, cut into 1-inch pieces

2 bell peppers, diced

1 (28-ounce) can of low sodium diced tomatoes

2 tablespoons of tomato paste

6 cups low sodium broth

2 bay leaves

Pepper

1/2 teaspoon of basil

1/2 teaspoon of thyme

2 cups of sliced zucchini

2 cups of broccoli florets

Directions:

1. Coat a large pot with cooking spray and place on medium heat. Cook the garlic and onion until onion becomes slightly soft.

2. Add the cabbage, carrots and green beans. Cook for 5 minutes more.

3. Add the bell peppers, tomatoes with its juice, tomato paste bay leaves, broth, bay leaves, pepper, basil and thyme. Let simmer for 6-7 minutes.

4. Add the broccoli and zucchini then simmer for an extra 5 minutes or until the veggies soften.

5. Remove bay leaves and serve.

Nutrition per serving:

Calories: 99, fat: 2.8g, carbohydrates: 4.7g, proteins: 5.9g

Zucchini Chicken Soup

Servings: 8

Prep time: 10 minutes

Cook time: 20 minutes

Ingredients:

1 pound of chicken breasts, sliced thinly

1 tablespoon of olive oil

1/2 onion, chopped

1 1/2 tablespoons of green curry paste

1 jalapeno, chopped

2 garlic cloves, minced

1 (15-ounce) can of coconut or almond milk

6 cups of chicken broth

2 tablespoons of fish sauce

1 red pepper, thinly sliced

1/2 cup of cilantro, chopped

2 medium zucchini, spiralized

1 lime, cut into 8 wedges

Directions:

1. In a large pan, heat the oil on medium heat. Add the onions and sauté for about 5 minutes or until translucent.

2. Stir in the curry paste, jalapeno and garlic. Sauté for about 1 minute or until fragrant.

3. Add the coconut milk and broth the whisk until well combined. Allow to boil and turn down the heat to medium.

4. Add the fish sauce, red pepper and chicken. Allow to simmer for about 5 minutes until the chicken is cooked through. Add the cilantro and stir.

5. Divide the zucchini among 8 bowls and ladle the hot soup over.

6. Serve with a squeeze of lime.

Nutrition per serving:

Calories: 270, fat: 12.5g, carbohydrates: 8.9g, proteins: 24.4g

Mediterranean Chicken Sandwich

Servings: 4

Prep time: 15 minutes

Cook time: 6 minutes

Ingredients:

4 whole grain bread slices

4 teaspoons olive oil, divided

1 pound chicken breast cutlets

1 tablespoon olive oil

Pepper

Salt

2 teaspoons Italian seasoning

3 roma tomatoes, chopped

1/4 cup fresh basil, chopped

1 garlic clove, chopped

1/3 red onion, chopped

1 teaspoon balsamic vinegar

4 slices mozzarella cheese

Directions:

1. Preheat oven to 425 °F.

2. Arrange the bread in a baking pan and drizzle with 2 teaspoons of olive oil. Cook the bread in oven for 3-4 minutes or until crispy.

3. In a bowl, combine chicken with 1 tablespoon of olive oil, salt, pepper and Italian seasoning then set aside.

4. Heat a pan or grill over medium high heat; cook the chicken for 3-4 minutes on each side or until well cooked.

5. Meanwhile, add together tomatoes, basil, onion, garlic and vinegar in a bowl. Toss to combine.

6. To serve, add 1 to 2 cutlets to each bread slice and top with 1slice of cheese.

7. Add the vegetable mixture as toppings and serve immediately.

Nutrition per serving:

Calories: 362, fat: 17.2g, carbohydrates: 17.1g, proteins: 35.9g

Spinach Grilled Cheese

Servings: 2

Prep time: 10 minutes

Cook time: 20 minutes

Ingredients:

2 ciabatta rolls, halved

1/2 tablespoon of olive oil

1 garlic clove, minced

1/4 pound of frozen cut spinach

1 ounce of feta cheese

1 cup of shredded mozzarella cheese

A pinch of salt and pepper

Directions:

1. In a pan, add oil and sauté the garlic for 1-2 minutes on medium low heat or until it starts to become soft.

2. Add the spinach, increase the heat to medium and cook for 5 minutes or until the spinach has lost most of its moisture and is well heated.

3. Add pepper and salt to taste.

4. Scoop about ½ ounce of feta and ¼ cup of the mozzarella unto the bottom of each ciabatta half.

5. Evenly divide the spinach mixture between the two bottom bread halves.

6. Add an additional ¼ cup of mozzarella to each bottom ciabatta half.

7. Cover the sandwiches with the top ciabatta half and arrange them on a large skillet.

8. Cover the sandwiches with a metal plate that is not as wide as the skillet. Add a few inches of water to a large pot to make it heavy and place on the metal plate to press down the sandwiches.

9. Cook on medium low heat until sandwiches are crisp at the bottom.

10. Flip gently and set the plate and pot on top again; cook until cheese melts and other side is crisp.

Nutrition per serving:

Calories: 213, fat: 11g, carbohydrates: 18g, proteins: 10.8g

Quinoa With Beans

Servings: 4

Prep time: 5 minutes

Cook time: 25 minutes

Ingredients:

1 (15 oounce) can of black beans

1 cup of dry quinoa, rinsed

2 cups of water

1/4 cup of tomato sauce

1 tablespoon of tomato paste

2 garlic cloves, minced

1/2 red bell pepper, chopped

1 small onion, chopped

5 ounces of spinach

1/2 teaspoon of paprika

1 teaspoon of dried thyme

1 teaspoon of powdered chili

1 teaspoon of cumin

1/2 teaspoon of salt

1/2 teaspoon of pepper

Directions:

1. In a medium sauce pan, heat a little water on medium heat. Add the onions and garlic then cook for 3 to 4 minutes. Add the rest of the spices then cook for 1 to 2 minutes.

3. Add the tomato paste and the sauce, then cook for another 1 to 2 minutes.

4. Add the quinoa and water. Bring to a boil, reduce the heat to a simmer, cover and cook for 20 minutes, or until all the water dries up.

5. Meanwhile, heat a little water in a skillet. Add the bell pepper and cook for 5 minutes. Add the spinach and continue cooking until it wilts then set aside.

6. Drain the black beans and rinse.

7. Once the quinoa is done cooking, add the black beans, the bell pepper and the spinach then mix to combine. Enjoy!

Nutrition per serving:

Calories: 251, fat: 3.4g, carbohydrates: 45g, proteins: 12g

Garlic Roasted Lamb Chops

Servings: 6

Prep time: 10 minutes

Cook time: 15 minutes

Ingredients:

6 lamb chops, room temperature

2 tablespoons extra virgin olive oil

3 garlic cloves, crushed

2 anchovy fillets, minced

1/2 teaspoon cracked black pepper

1 teaspoon anchovy oil

Directions:

1. Preheat oven to 375°F.

2. In a small bowl, whisk the anchovies, black pepper, garlic and anchovy oil together.

3. Season the lamb with pepper and salt lightly.

4. Brush both sides of the lamb chops with the garlic and oil mixture.

5. In a large pan, heat oil on medium high heat and sauté the lamb chops for 2-3 minutes per side; transfer cooked chops to a roasting pan.

6. Roast the lamb chops in the oven for about 13-15 minutes.

Nutrition per serving:

Calories: 364, fat: 30.9g, carbohydrates: 0g, proteins: 19.6g

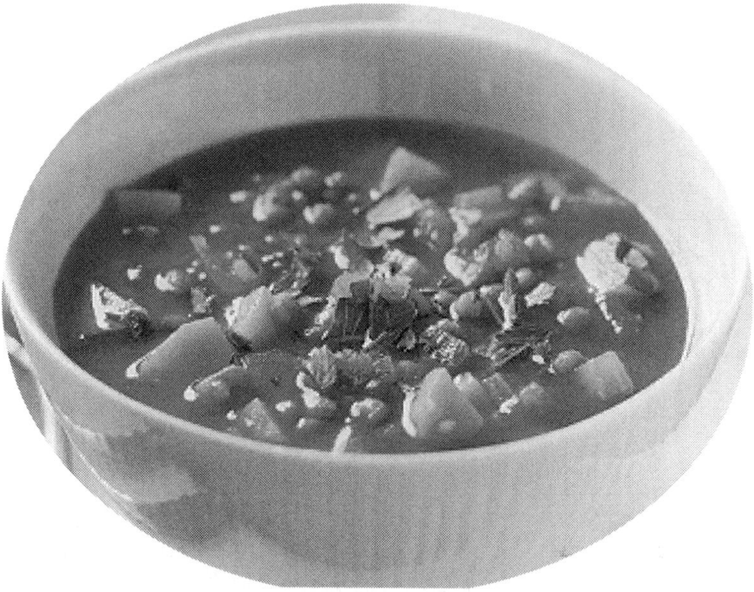

Lentil Vegetable Soup

Servings: 8

Prep time: 20 minutes

Cook time: 40 minutes

Ingredients:

2 tablespoons olive oil

2 large carrots, peeled, chopped

1 small onion, diced

5 garlic cloves, minced

2 teaspoons cumin

1/2 teaspoon dried thyme

1 (15 oz) can chickpeas, drained, rinsed

2 (15 oz) cans fire roasted diced tomatoes

1 cup green lentils

3 cups water

4 cups vegetable stock

2 cups kale, ribs removed, chopped

1 teaspoon pepper

1 teaspoon salt

1/2 teaspoon red pepper flakes

Directions:

1. In a large pot, heat oil on medium heat and sauté the carrots and onion with frequent stirring until onion is opaque and soft.

2. Add thyme, garlic and cumin and sauté until aromatic.

3. Stir in the chickpeas, fire roasted tomatoes, lentils, water and stock.

4. Add red pepper flakes, salt and pepper.

5. Allow the soup to come to a boil then lower the heat to a gentle simmer.

6. Cook for about 30 minutes or until lentils are softened.

7. Scoop about 3 cups of the soup into a food processor or blender and pulse until smooth.

8. Return the processed mixture to the pot and add the kale. Cook until kale wilts.

Nutrition per serving:

Calories: 348, fat: 7.3g, carbohydrates: 55g, proteins: 18.4g

Vegetable Stir Fry

Servings: 6

Prep time: 25 minutes

Cook time: 15 minutes

Ingredients:

1 small head broccoli, cut into florets

3/4 cup carrots, julienned

1/2 cup green beans, halved

1/2 cup snow peas

1/4 cup chopped onion

1/4 cup olive oil, divided

1 tablespoon cornstarch

1 1/2 garlic cloves, crushed

2 teaspoon chopped fresh ginger root

2 1/2 tablespoon water

2 tablespoon fish sauce

1/2 teaspoon salt

Directions:

1. Add together 2 tablespoons of oil, the cornstarch, ginger and garlic in a large bowl then whisk until the cornstarch has dissolved. Add all the vegetables and toss to coat.

2. In a large skillet, add the remaining oil and heat on medium heat. Add the vegetables then cook and stir constantly for 2 minutes.

3. Pour in the water and fish sauce. Sprinkle with salt and stir. Cook until the vegetables have become crisp tender.

Nutrition per serving:

Calories: 119, fat: 9.4g, carbohydrates: 8g, proteins: 2.4g

Penned With Asparagus, Leeks And Tomatoes

Servings: 6

Prep time: 15 minutes

Cook time: 40 minutes

Ingredients:

8 ounces uncooked whole wheat penne

2 pounds uncooked asparagus

6 cups of cherry tomatoes

2 medium uncooked leeks

2 tablespoons of extra virgin olive oil

1 teaspoon of kosher salt

1/2 cup of chopped basil

1/4 teaspoon of black pepper

1 teaspoon of lemon zest

1 teaspoon of minced garlic

Salt

Shredded parmigiano reggiano cheese

Directions:

1. Preheat oven to 375°F.

2. Grease 2 rimmed baking sheets with nonstick cooking spray.

3. Add the asparagus, tomatoes, oil, leeks, pepper and salt to the pans and toss together; evenly spread the veggies in the baking sheets.

4. Roast for about 35-40 minutes, stirring just once, halfway through the cooking time.

5. Boil a large pot of salted water and cook the penne following instructions on the package. When done, reserve ¼ cup of the pasta liquid then drain the pasta.

6. Add the roasted veggies, pasta, reserved cooking liquid, garlic, lemon zest and garlic to a large bowl; toss together.

7. Serve with a garnish of cheese.

Nutrition per serving:

Calories: 276, fat: 7.5g, carbohydrates: 45g, proteins: 13g

Roasted Chicken And Spinach Salad

Servings: 6

Prep time: 10 minutes

Cook time: 1 hour

Ingredients:

1 small whole chicken

1/2 cup of olive oil

4 teaspoons of lemon juice

1 1/2 teaspoons of paprika

1 tablespoon of grated ginger

3 garlic cloves

1 1/2 teaspoons of yellow curry powder

1 1/2 teaspoons of coriander

1 1/2 teaspoons of cumin

1/2 teaspoon of crushed red pepper flakes

1 bunches parsley with stems, roughly chopped

6 cups of spinach

1 tablespoon extra virgin olive oil

1/4 small red onion, thinly sliced

2 tablespoons capers

1/4 cup pecorino

Black pepper

Kosher salt

Directions:

1. Preheat oven to 400°F.

2. Pulse the ½ cup olive oil, paprika, ginger, garlic, curry powder, cumin, red pepper flakes, coriander, and 1 teaspoon of lemon juice in a blender on low for 1 minute.

3. Add the parsley and pulse until mixture is bright green and smooth. Add salt and pepper to taste.

4. Rub the marinade all over the chicken.

5. Roast chicken in oven for 45 to 60 minutes or until inner temperature at the thigh's thickest part reads 165°F. Remove from oven when done and leave to sit for 5 minutes.

6. In a bowl, combine the capers, red onion, spinach, and the extra virgin olive oil and lemon juice together.

7. Add the pecorino as toppings on the salad.

8. Serve the salad with the chicken.

Nutrition per serving:

Calories: 204, fat: 18.8g, carbohydrates: 2.4g, proteins: 8.1g

Chickpea Vegetable Curry

This delicious meal is ready in less than one hour. You can serve it with quinoa or brown rice if you like.

Servings: 6

Prep Time: 10 minutes

Cook Time: 40 minutes

Ingredients:

4 garlic cloves, minced

1/2 a medium white onion, chopped

1 tablespoon olive oil

1 bell pepper, chopped

2 cups broccoli florets

1 small butternut squash, cubed

1 (15 ounce) can chickpeas

1 (15 ounce) can diced tomatoes

3 cups low sodium vegetable broth

1 (14.5 ounce) can lite coconut milk

1/2 teaspoon turmeric

1/4 teaspoon cinnamon

2 teaspoons curry

3/4 teaspoon coriander

1 teaspoon cumin

Salt, to taste

Pepper, to taste

Cilantro to garnish

Directions:

1. In a large saucepan, heat the oil on medium heat. Add garlic and onion and sauté for about 4 minutes.

2. Add the bell pepper, broccoli, butternut squash and chickpeas. Cook and stir for 2 minutes more.

3. Pour in the diced tomatoes, vegetable broth, coconut milk, turmeric, cinnamon, curry, coriander, cumin, salt and pepper.

4. Bring to a boil then reduce to a simmer, cover and cook for 30 minutes or until the squash is tender.

5. Serve in bowls and garnish with cilantro.

Nutrition per serving:

Calories: 197, fat: 6g, carbohydrates: 28g, proteins: 6g

Shrimp With Brown Rice

This comes together easily and it is very tasty.

Servings: 4

Prep Time: 15 minutes

Cook Time: 20 minutes

Ingredients:

1 cup of brown rice

1 2/3 cups of water

4 - 5 tablespoons olive oil

2 garlic cloves, minced

2 tablespoons fresh lemon juice

1/2 cup white wine

1 1/2 pounds of medium shrimp, peeled, deveined

1/4 cup of chopped fresh parsley

1/2 teaspoon cornstarch

Directions:

1. In a small saucepan, combine the brown rice with the water medium high heat. When it starts boiling, reduce to low heat, cover and cook until the rice has absorbed the water, about 25 minutes. Remove from heat and set aside.

2. In a skillet, heat the oil on medium heat. Add the garlic and cook for 1 to 2 minutes to release its fragrance. Pour in the lemon juice and white wine, reduce to medium-low heat and let simmer.

3. Stir in the shrimp then continue cooking, stirring regularly for 5 to 7 minutes, or until the shrimp is pink.

4. Add the parsley and cook for 2 minutes more.

6. Stir the cornstarch into the liquid to thicken then allow to heat through.

7. Serve with the cooked brown rice.

Nutrition per serving:

Calories: 545, fat: 23g, carbohydrates: 40g, proteins: 39g

SNACKS & APPETIZERS

Easy Dip

This dip is also great with fruits and veggies.

Servings: 3-4

Prep time: 5 minutes

Cook time: 0 minutes

Ingredients:

1 cup of crumbled feta

1/4 cup of sun-dried tomato

1/3 cup of diced kalamata olives

2 tablespoons of diced flat leaf parsley

2 tablespoons of diced fresh oregano

1 1/2 teaspoons of lime juice

1 tablespoon of olive oil

1 tablespoon of chopped green onions

Fresh ground pepper, to taste

Crackers

Directions:

1. In a small bowl, add all the ingredients and mix well.

2. Serve with the crackers.

Nutrition per serving:

Calories: 152, fat: 12.3g, carbohydrates: 3.6g, proteins: 7.4g

Mediterranean Guacamole

This makes a great spread on toast.

Servings: 8

Prep time: 10 minutes

Cook time: 0 minutes

Ingredients:

1/4 cup of diced red onion

4 whole kalamata olives, pitted, chopped

2 large ripe avocados, pitted, halved

3 tablespoons of diced ripe cherry tomato

1 heaping tablespoon of chopped sun-dried tomatoes

2 tablespoons of lemon juice

2 tablespoons of fresh chopped parsley

1 teaspoon of dried oregano

1/8 teaspoon black pepper

1/8 teaspoon sea salt

Directions:

1. In a large bowl, mash the lemon juice and avocado with a large fork or potato masher.

2. Stir in the rest of the ingredients.

3. Taste and adjust seasoning if needed.

Nutrition per serving:

Calories: 110, fat: 10g, carbohydrates: 5.7g, proteins: 1.2g

Pistachios Bars

Servings: 8

Prep time: 20 minutes

Cook time: 0 minutes

Ingredients:

20 dates, pitted

1 cup of rolled old fashioned oats

1 1/4 cups of no-shell roasted and salted pistachios, divided

1/4 cup of unsweetened applesauce

2 tablespoons of pistachio butter

1 teaspoon of vanilla extract

Directions:

1. Line a baking pan with parchment paper.

2. Pulse the dates in a food processor for about 30-45 seconds.

3. Add the oats and 1 cup of pistachios; pulse for 15 seconds, about 2-3 times, until mixture is coarse and crumbly.

4. Add the vanilla extract, applesauce and pistachio butter to the food processor and process for 20-30 seconds until the mixture is a bit sticky.

5. Remove from the food processor with a spatula unto the prepared pan.

6. Use another parchment paper to firmly press down on the mixture so it is distributed evenly in the pan.

7. Remove the paper and sprinkle the remaining pistachios on the mixture.

8. Cover again with the parchment paper and freeze for an hour or more before slicing.

9. Cut into 8 squares.

Nutrition per serving:

Calories: 220, fat: 12g, carbohydrates: 26g, proteins: 6g

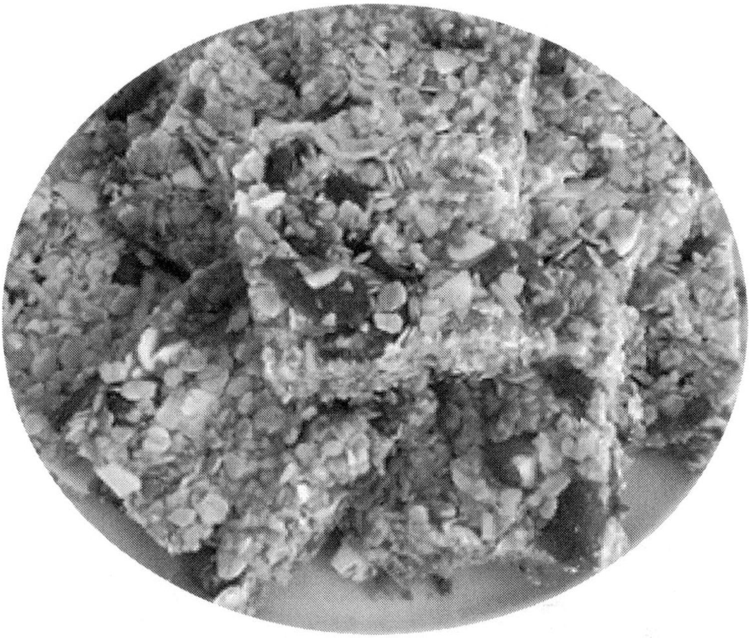

Fruity Almond Butter Oat Bars

This gives you a nutritious snack for several days.

Servings: 24

Prep time: 10 minutes

Cook time: minutes

Ingredients:

2 1/2 cups rolled oats

1 1/4 cups creamy almond butter

1/3 cup of chopped raw unsalted almonds

1/2 cup chopped unsweetened dried apple

1/2 cup unsweetened dried cranberries

1/2 cup raw honey

2 teaspoons of whole flaxseeds

1/3 cup ground flaxseeds

1/2 teaspoon ground cinnamon

Directions:

1. Add all the ingredients to a large bowl and mix together with a spoon until fully combined.

2. Wet your hands and press the mixture into an 8 by 8 inch baking dish.

3. Place in the fridge for 3 to 4 hours until it hardens

4. Use a knife to cut into 24 bars. Wrap in waxed paper and store in the fridge for up to a week.

Nutrition per serving:

Calories: 159, fat: 9g, carbohydrates: 18g, proteins: 4g

Chocolate Cookie Snack Balls

Every bite of these nutty and chewy balls is delicious.

Servings: 26

Prep time: 20 minutes

Cook time: minutes

Ingredients:

3/4 cup unsweetened flaked coconut

1 1/4 cups rolled oats

2 tablespoons coconut oil

5 tablespoons raw honey

3/4 cup peanut butter

1 teaspoon vanilla extract

1/2 cup of dark chocolate chips

Shredded coconut for topping

Directions:

1. Line a large baking sheet with parchment paper.

2. Combine coconut flakes and rolled oats in a food processor and pulse for about 30 seconds or until coarsely ground.

3. Add the coconut oil, honey, peanut butter and vanilla. Pulse for 30 seconds more until the mixture is well combined.

4. Add the chocolate chips, pulse a few more times to combine. Scoop the mixture into a bowl.

5. Wet your hands and take about 1 tablespoon of the dough and form it into a ball. Roll the ball in the shredded coconut and place on the prepared baking sheet. Repeat until you are out of dough.

6. Place in the refrigerator to chill for at least 2 hours. Transfer to an airtight container and store in the fridge for up to 1 week.

Nutrition per serving:

Calories: 131, fat: 9g, carbohydrates: 11g, proteins: 2g

Julienned Apple With Chocolate

Servings: 3

Prep Time: 5 minutes

Cook Time: 10 minutes

Ingredients:

3 apples, julienned

3 tablespoons coconut oil

4 tablespoons of cacao

3 tablespoons of maple syrup

Directions:

1. Combine cacao and coconut oil in a pot and place on low heat. Cook and stir for about 5 minutes until the mixture has melted completely.

2. Remove from heat and immediately stir in maple syrup.

3. Divide the apple strips among serving plates. Top each dish with the melted chocolate sauce.

Nutrition per serving:

Calories: 275, fat: 14g, carbohydrates: 38g, proteins: 1g

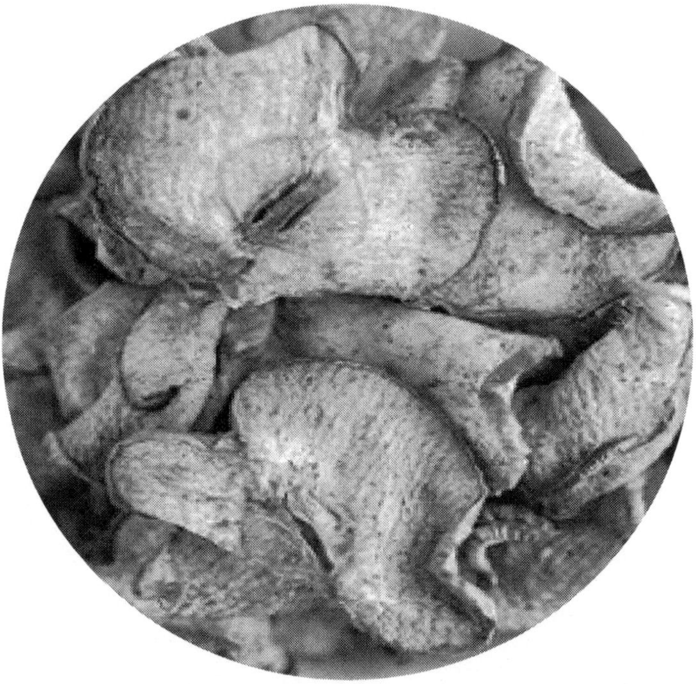

Cinnamon Apple Chips

This is much better than what you will get in a store.

Servings: 6

Prep time: 20 minutes

Cook time: 2 hours 30 minutes

Ingredients:

3 large sweet apples, cored, sliced (1/8 inch thick)

3/4 teaspoon of ground cinnamon

Directions:

1. Preheat the oven to 200°F. Place parchment paper on two baking sheets.

2. On the prepared baking sheets, spread out the apple slices in a single layer and sprinkle with cinnamon.

3. Bake in the oven for 60 minutes. Swith the positions of the baking sheets and bake for additional 60 to 90 minutes or until the apple slices are crisp.

Nutrition per serving:

Calories: 65, fat: g, carbohydrates: 18g, proteins: g

Garlic Herb Marinated Olives

Servings: 4

Prep time: 10 minutes

Cook time: 5 minutes

Ingredients:

1/4 cup extra virgin olive oil

2 garlic cloves, crushed

Zest of half a lemon

1 sprig fresh rosemary, leaves torn from the stem

3 sprigs fresh thyme

1/4 teaspoon dried fennel seeds

1/4 teaspoon ground cumin

1 1/2 cups mixed olives

Directions:

1. Add the oil to a skillet and heat on medium low heat. Add garlic, lemon zest, rosemary, thyme, fennel seeds and cumin. Cook and stir until the herbs are fragrant, about 2 to 3 minutes.

2. Add the olives then toss to coat and let it warm through.

3. Remove from the heat and transfer to a jar and let it cool.

4. You can store in the fridge for up to 3 days. Reheat gently when you want to serve.

Nutrition per serving:

Calories: 210, fat: 21g, carbohydrates: 6g, proteins: 1g

Spicy Roasted Almonds

This is a crunchy delight with very rich flavor.

Servings: 32

Prep time: 5 minutes

Cook time: 10 minutes

Ingredients:

2 cups whole almonds

1 tablespoon extra-virgin olive oil

1 tablespoon chili powder

1/4 teaspoon freshly ground black pepper

1/2 teaspoon kosher salt

1/4 teaspoon ground cinnamon

1/2 teaspoon ground coriander

1/2 teaspoon ground cumin

Directions:

1. Preheat your oven to 350°F.

2. In a medium bowl, mix together olive oil, chili powder, black pepper, salt, cinnamon, coriander and cumin.

3. Add the almonds and mix until coated. Transfer to a large baking pan.

4. Bake and stir occasionally until the almonds are toasted, about 10 minutes.

5. Remove from the oven and let cool before serving. You can store in an airtight container for 4 to 5 days.

Nutrition per serving:

Calories: 57, fat: 5g, carbohydrates: 2g, proteins: 2g

Chicken Tenders With Herbs

Servings: 6

Prep time: 10 minutes

Cook time: 10 minutes

Ingredients:

1 pound chicken breast tenders

2 tablespoons olive oil

6 sprigs fresh thyme, chopped

1 garlic clove, minced

1/4 cup lemon juice

1 tablespoon lemon zest

Salt, to taste

Pepper, to taste

Olive oil cooking spray

Directions:

1. In a large bowl, mix together olive oil, thyme, garlic, lemon juice and lemon zest.

2. Rub the chicken all over with salt and pepper. Add the chicken to the olive oil mixture and toss to coat. Set aside to marinate for 10 minutes.

3. Spray cooking spray on a skillet and place it on medium high heat. Add the chicken and cook for about 4 minutes per side or until browned and cooked through.

Nutrition per serving:

Calories: 128, fat: 6.4g, carbohydrates: 1.3g, proteins: 15.8g

END

Made in the USA
Monee, IL
21 September 2020